LEGISLATURES

Published in association with the Centre for Canadian Studies at Mount Allison University. Information on the Canadian Democratic Audit project can be found at www.CanadianDemocraticAudit.ca.

Advisory Group

William Cross, Director (Mount Allison University)
R. Kenneth Carty (University of British Columbia)
Elisabeth Gidengil (McGill University)
Richard Sigurdson (University of New Brunswick)
Frank Strain (Mount Allison University)
Michael Tucker (Mount Allison University)

Titles

John Courtney, *Elections*
William Cross, *Political Parties*
Elisabeth Gidengil, André Blais, Neil Nevitte, and Richard Nadeau, *Citizens*
Jennifer Smith, *Federalism*
Lisa Young and Joanna Everitt, *Advocacy Groups*
David Docherty, *Legislatures*
Darin Barney, *Communications Technology*
Graham White, *Cabinets and First Ministers*
Ian Greene, *The Courts*

LEGISLATURES

David C. Docherty

UBCPress

15 14 13 12 11 10 09 08 07 06 05   5 4 3 2 1

Printed in Canada on acid-free paper that is 100% post-consumer recycled, processed chlorine-free, and printed with vegetable-based, low-VOC inks.

Library and Archives Canada Cataloguing in Publication

Docherty, David Campbell, 1961-
  Legislatures / David C. Docherty.

  (Canadian democratic audit; 6)
  Includes bibliographical references and index.
  ISBN 0-7748-1101-3 (set). – ISBN 0-7748-1064-5 (bound); ISBN 0-7748-1065-3 (pbk)

  1. Legislative bodies – Canada. I. Title. II. Series: Canadian democratic audit.

JL136.D62 2005   328.71   C2004-905862-2

Canadä

UBC Press gratefully acknowledges the financial support for our publishing program of the Government of Canada through the Book Publishing Industry Development Program (BPIDP), and of the Canada Council for the Arts and the British Columbia Arts Council.

The Centre for Canadian Studies thanks the Harold Crabtree Foundation for its support of the Canadian Democratic Audit project.

This book has been published with the help of the K.D. Srivastava Fund.

UBC Press
The University of British Columbia
2029 West Mall
Vancouver, BC V6T 1Z2
604-822-5959 / Fax: 604-822-6083
www.ubcpress.ca

CONTENTS

Tables

FOREWORD

This volume is part of the Canadian Democratic Audit series. The objective of this series is to consider how well Canadian democracy is performing at the outset of the twenty-first century. In recent years, political and opinion leaders, government commissions, academics, citizen groups, and the popular press have all identified a "democratic deficit" and "democratic malaise" in Canada. These characterizations often are portrayed as the result of a substantial decline in Canadians' confidence in their democratic practices and institutions. Indeed, Canadians are voting in record low numbers, many are turning away from the traditional political institutions, and a large number are expressing declining confidence in both their elected politicians and the electoral process.

Nonetheless, Canadian democracy continues to be the envy of much of the rest of the world. Living in a relatively wealthy and peaceful society, Canadians hold regular elections in which millions cast ballots. These elections are largely fair, efficient, and orderly events. They routinely result in the selection of a government with no question about its legitimate right to govern. Developing democracies from around the globe continue to look to Canadian experts for guidance in establishing electoral practices and democratic institutions. Without a doubt, Canada is widely seen as a leading example of successful democratic practice.

Given these apparently competing views, the time is right for a comprehensive examination of the state of Canadian democracy. Our purposes are to conduct a systematic review of the operations of Canadian democracy, to listen to what others have to say about Canadian democracy, to assess its strengths and weaknesses, to consider where there are opportunities for advancement, and to evaluate popular reform proposals.

A democratic audit requires the setting of benchmarks for evaluation of the practices and institutions to be considered. This necessarily involves substantial consideration of the meaning of democracy.

"Democracy" is a contested term and we are not interested here in striking a definitive definition. Nor are we interested in a theoretical model applicable to all parts of the world. Rather we are interested in identifying democratic benchmarks relevant to Canada in the twenty-first century. In selecting these we were guided by the issues raised in the current literature on Canadian democratic practice and by the concerns commonly raised by opinion leaders and found in public opinion data. We have settled on three benchmarks: public participation, inclusiveness, and responsiveness. We believe that any contemporary definition of Canadian democracy must include institutions and decision-making practices that are defined by public participation, that this participation must include all Canadians, and that government outcomes must respond to the views of Canadians.

While settling on these guiding principles, we have not imposed a strict set of democratic criteria on all of the evaluations that together constitute the Audit. Rather, our approach allows the auditors wide latitude in their evaluations. While all auditors keep the benchmarks of participation, inclusiveness, and responsiveness central to their examinations, each adds additional criteria of particular importance to the subject he or she is considering. We believe this approach of identifying unifying themes, while allowing for divergent perspectives, enhances the project by capturing the robustness of the debate surrounding democratic norms and practices.

We decided at the outset to cover substantial ground and to do so in a relatively short period. These two considerations, coupled with a desire to respond to the most commonly raised criticisms of the contemporary practice of Canadian democracy, result in a series that focuses on public institutions, electoral practices, and new phenomena that are likely to affect democratic life significantly. The series includes volumes that examine key public decision-making bodies: legislatures, the courts, and cabinets and government. The structures of our democratic system are considered in volumes devoted to questions of federalism and the electoral system. The ways in which citizens participate in electoral politics and policy making are a crucial component of the project, and thus we include studies of interest groups and political parties. The desire and capacity of Canadians for meaningful participation in public life is also the subject of a volume. Finally, the challenges and opportunities raised by new communication technologies are also considered. The Audit does not include studies devoted to the status of particular groups of Canadians. Rather than separate out Aboriginals, women, new Canadians, and others, these groups are treated together with all Canadians throughout the Audit.

In all, this series includes nine volumes examining specific areas of Canadian democratic life. A tenth, synthetic volume provides an overall assessment and makes sense out of the different approaches and findings found in the rest of the series. Our examination is not exhaustive. Canadian democracy is a vibrant force, the status of which can never be fully captured at one time. Nonetheless the areas we consider involve many of the pressing issues currently facing democracy in Canada. We do not expect to have the final word on this subject. Rather, we hope to encourage others to pursue similar avenues of inquiry.

A project of this scope cannot be accomplished without the support of many individuals. At the top of the list of those deserving credit are the members of the Canadian Democratic Audit team. From the very beginning, the Audit has been a team effort. This outstanding group of academics has spent many hours together, defining the scope of the project, prodding each other on questions of Canadian democracy, and most importantly, supporting one another throughout the endeavour, all with good humour. To Darin Barney, André Blais, Kenneth Carty, John Courtney, David Docherty, Joanna Everitt, Elisabeth Gidengil, Ian Greene, Richard Nadeau, Neil Nevitte, Richard Sigurdson, Jennifer Smith, Frank Strain, Michael Tucker, Graham White, and Lisa Young I am forever grateful.

The Centre for Canadian Studies at Mount Allison University has been my intellectual home for several years. The Centre, along with the Harold Crabtree Foundation, has provided the necessary funding and other assistance necessary to see this project through to fruition. At Mount Allison University, Peter Ennals provided important support to this project when others were skeptical; Wayne MacKay and Michael

Fox have continued this support since their respective arrivals on campus; and Joanne Goodrich and Peter Loewen have provided important technical and administrative help.

The University of British Columbia Press, particularly its senior acquisitions editor, Emily Andrew, has been a partner in this project from the very beginning. Emily has been involved in every important decision and has done much to improve the result. Camilla Gurdon has overseen the copyediting and production process and in doing so has made these books better. Scores of Canadian and international political scientists have participated in the project as commentators at our public conferences, as critics at our private meetings, as providers of quiet advice, and as referees of the volumes. The list is too long to name them all, but David Cameron, Sid Noel, Leslie Seidle, Jim Bickerton, Alexandra Dobrowolsky, Livianna Tossutti, Janice Gross Stein, and Frances Abele all deserve special recognition for their contributions. We are also grateful to the Canadian Study of Parliament Group, which partnered with us for our inaugural conference in Ottawa in November 2001.

Finally, this series is dedicated to all of the men and women who contribute to the practice of Canadian democracy. Whether as active participants in parties, groups, courts, or legislatures, or in the media and the universities, without them Canadian democracy would not survive.

William Cross
Director, The Canadian Democratic Audit
Sackville, New Brunswick

Acknowledgments

It is a rare treat to be invited to participate in a large research program that exposes you to experts in all fields of Canadian politics. The Democratic Audit project has allowed a number of Canadian political scientists to meet regularly for over two years. Although the original design of the project did not call for new research, the energy and ideas generated by these meetings led most of us to broaden our initial foci and look at our projects in fresh ways. For my part this meant making extensive use of a Social Sciences and Humanities Research Council of Canada standard research grant, which allowed me to hire research assistants to collect data on all fifteen legislatures in Canada. I thank SSHRC for its continued support of social science research in Canada. I would also like to thank the following students for their assistance: Mark Labenksi, Emily Bain, Julie Hare, Jay Barber, and Sarah Roberts. I thank the two anonymous reviewers for their helpful comments. Thanks also to Graham White and Gary Levy, who made comments on earlier parts of this book, and to the Parliamentary Information and Research Service for answering my many queries.

I would like to thank Bill Cross at Mount Allison University for spearheading such a mammoth undertaking. It was a pleasure to be involved in the Audit project. Joanne Goodrich at Mount Allison was of tremendous assistance to all of us with travel arrangements, logistical support, and general goodwill – thanks, Joanne. As with my past experience with UBC Press, I was blown away by the level of professionalism and assistance of this publisher. Ken Carty, Emily Andrew, and Camilla Gurdon have helped make the task of writing a book much more pleasurable than one might imagine.

Finally, I would like to thank Sarah, Angus, and Quinn for their patience and understanding. They never complained when I feigned anguish at having to travel to New Brunswick or Ottawa or Halifax or Toronto to meet my Audit colleagues. And of course, they saw right through my protestations, as they knew I relished the chance to spend time with such a fine group of academics.

Legislatures

A DEMOCRATIC AUDIT
OF CANADIAN LEGISLATURES

1

Legislatures, and the men and women who serve in them, are at the very heart of Canadian democracy. After all, with the exception of two nationwide referenda in Canada last century, Canadians speak collectively only when they vote to select the person who will be representing their interests in Ottawa. The same is true provincially. While there have been a handful more referenda in some jurisdictions, members of provincial assemblies, and by extension the assemblies themselves, remain the focal points of democracy.

But how democratic are legislative assemblies in Canada? After we elect our representatives, are we comfortable that we are being properly, and democratically, represented? Apparently not, for legislatures at the provincial and national levels seem to be wallowing in new lows of public approval ratings. Members of federal and provincial parliaments are consistently ranked lower, i.e., as less trustworthy, than courts, where justices are appointed and little is known of members of the bench. The second most successful national party in the past fifteen years – the Reform/Alliance – elected members by running against Parliament. Somehow we elect legislators, give governments high approval ratings, and simultaneously consider politicians and Parliament to be beneath contempt. We elect people with certain expectations, and when they are not met we hold those people, and the institution in which they serve, responsible.

Why are legislatures and legislators failing to meet public expectations in Canada? Several explanations are possible. First, we may be electing the wrong people. This is the problem of personnel: the men and women who win elections may not be capable of properly representing Canadians. Second, our legislatures may not be configured in such a manner as to provide us with the type of representation we seek. This is the problem of institutional design: our legislatures are designed to perform certain functions, but they might not be the functions we wish them to perform. Third, the reason may be a combination of the first two explanations: we might be exacerbating the problem of institutional design by electing the wrong people to office. Fourth and finally, it may be that legislatures do perform some functions well but that these functions are seen as less important than functions the parliament does less well. Simply put, most voters expect elected members to represent their interests in Ottawa. Yet most members are elected with fewer than half the votes in their riding, and views of constituents are rarely, if ever, unanimous. Even if a legislator could properly gauge the majority of local sentiment, on all but the most important issues party solidarity can prohibit the member from placing riding above party. Duties that legislatures do encourage, such as effective committee work and one-on-one constituency service, are well below the public radar.

This book provides a democratic audit of Canada's provincial and national representative assemblies. It argues that the problem existing in these bodies is not necessarily a lack of talent (though the incentive structure to entice quality candidates could be improved) so much as a lack of institutional freedom. Parliament may be capable of performing the traditional duties of a Westminster assembly, but many of these are not the duties that Canadians see as important in a modern democracy. The move to a multiparty system nationally, and the tendency to downsize provincial assemblies, have created additional hurdles to good governance in Canada.

The problems of institutional freedom and size are compounded by a lack of public appreciation for the strengths of representation in

Canada. Some of the true success stories of modern legislatures and legislators are those very things that do not rank high on the public's list of priorities, but are nonetheless essential to good governance in a democratic state. In sum, legislatures are overburdened. Members are restricted from engaging in some activities that the public thinks are important, and at the same time compelled to expend effort in activities that do not receive appropriate publicity. Further, there is a disjuncture between what parliamentary systems are designed to do and what the public, and increasingly members, think they can and should do. The result is a recipe for public disappointment and a group of frustrated legislators. How do students of government, interested participants, and citizens in general make sense of this?

One method is to establish some criteria for the performance of legislatures. Until we delineate what functions they should be performing, it is difficult to hold representative bodies up to any type of standard. Just as important, we must recognize that there are some tasks that a legislature should not perform. Calls for reform may be passionate and well meaning, but if they are not undertaken with an understanding about the basic needs of all citizens for representation – or a realistic understanding of the likelihood of comprehensive institutional renewal – then intended reforms may have unintended consequences.

The Democratic Audit series relies on three benchmarks to guide the audits of institutions and aspects of governance in Canada: responsiveness, inclusiveness, and participation. Before delimiting the functional criteria that will guide this audit, we begin with a brief description of how these three themes relate to questions of representation and legislative arrangements in Canada.

Responsiveness

Democratic institutions should be responsive institutions. This begs the obvious question, responsive to what or to whom? Certainly some assemblies, or representative systems, are more capable of quick reactions to public demands, while others favour slower, more deliberate debate and consensus prior to any legislative or policy action (Atkinson 1994). Aside from responsiveness to the public, there is another traditional parliamentary understanding of what constitutes responsiveness: a government that acts knowing it is always at risk of losing internal support. Institutions can be responsive both to external, public pressures and to internal demands.

This latter understanding of responsiveness has characterized our appreciation of parliamentary systems. Jennifer Smith (1998) has argued that parliamentary governments are the most responsive of all systems. The constant requirement for confidence of the party and the House means that a prime minister must always be vigilant. The lack of fixed terms allows snap elections if the government loses a vote of confidence or a vote on other types of legislation.

This form of responsiveness, however, is more apparent in theory than in reality. Westminster parliaments are typified by high levels of party discipline. Concerns over maintaining confidence between elections are never close to the forefront of prime ministerial concerns. This is particularly true in Canada, where majority governments have become more commonplace. The 2004 vote produced the first minority government in a quarter century, since Joe Clark was prime minister in 1979-80. Canada does have an increasing number of political parties, and multiparty parliaments are more conducive to minority governments. At least in the short term, however, these parties are increasingly regionalized (Carty, Cross, and Young 2000, 34). The net effect of new parties has been to reinforce majority governments, not challenge their existence.

Nor have provincial governments been faced with a compelling need to be responsive to their caucus or opposition. Party discipline in the provincial assemblies is every bit as strong as nationally. Further, many provinces effectively operate with two-party systems (or in the case of Alberta, a near one-party state). Only half the provinces have something approximating a three-party system.

This lack of internal responsiveness is an important deficiency in Canadian legislatures. There has never been a strong period of internal responsiveness in Canadian parliamentary history. As C.E.S. Franks (1987) indicates, the golden age of Parliament never really existed.

However, the lack of internal responsiveness currently appears to be at an all-time low. The power of the executive is increasingly drawn further inward to the Prime Minister's Office. Not only are decisions becoming more centralized (not a direct measure of unresponsiveness) but central actors perceive no need to consult or respond to their own elected members (see Savoie 1999).

In terms of external responsiveness, the required infrastructure for providing responsive governance is in place. Further, members of legislatures are generally inclined to seek out opinions of citizens, particularly those affected by intended legislative changes. This contact can occur through the committee stage of legislation. Additionally, critics for ministers have an extensive network of interested parties they regularly contact. Yet the ability to act on citizen input is compromised by the problem of internal responsiveness cited above. Governments have little impetus to react to the legislature.

This is not to argue that governments are not responsive to citizen demands. Indeed, the last quarter-century in Canada has witnessed some dramatic changes aimed at increasing democratic responsiveness. The patriation of the Constitution, and specifically the establishment of the Charter of Rights and Freedoms, were seen by many as the democratic coming of age of Canada (See Cairns 1992, ch. 1). Recent moves by provincial governments on Aboriginal concerns, such as the Nisga'a Treaty in British Columbia, also illustrate that governments can be responsive. Legislatures are not necessarily an efficient vehicle for responsiveness. In fact, given the nature of parliamentary government and the role of the opposition to question government activities one could argue that legislatures are better agents of blocking responsiveness than of facilitating change. Despite the weakness of internal responsiveness, the opposition and government private members have a number of avenues available to bring public sentiment to the attention of members of the cabinet. Question period, committee hearings, members' statements, caucus, press releases, and conferences cannot make the executive respond. But they are designed to draw attention to issues and often increase public (and government) awareness of public policy concerns.

Inclusiveness

Inclusiveness suggests that institutions or organizations try to ensure that certain segments of society are not excluded from becoming a member of the group. A male-only club is exclusive, in that females are not allowed to join. Canadian public institutions forbid most formal exclusiveness. The problem is that informal barriers to inclusiveness also affect who is elected to office in Canada.

The formal barriers are simply the rules saying who is eligible (and thus who is ineligible) to serve in office. Originally, only landowning males in Canada were permitted to vote and run for office. This is exclusivity at its highest form. Women were first allowed to vote in the 1917 election if they or their husbands, sons, brothers, or fathers were in the armed services. The original extension of the franchise to women, therefore, was not undertaken to recognize their right to vote but to increase support for the war effort. Once granted, however, it was impossible not to extend the vote to all women, which occurred nationally in 1921.

We still legislate some exclusiveness in legislatures in Canada. The most obvious factor is age. At present, one must be eighteen years of age to vote and to serve in the House of Commons or provincial assemblies. Recent debate has suggested lowering the minimum age to sixteen, but no moves have been made in that direction. The rationale for an age bar is maturity. While many Canadians aged sixteen and seventeen are probably more mature and reflective than some adults, this is more relevant to the question of the vote (covered by John Courtney's audit [2004]) than to the ability to serve. Fitness to serve also involves experience. Although youth should have a voice in Canada's Parliament, that voice may not come most appropriately from individuals who have only had experience being young. The Senate has an even higher age bar: only those thirty and older may serve.

The informal aspect of inclusiveness is not legal or restrictive. Who serves in office? The basket of those eligible to serve is much bigger than the number chosen to serve, either by Canadians or by the prime minister. Historically, the Canadian Parliament has tended to over-represent certain demographic segments of society. White men continue to dominate the assembly, though Parliament is now far less white and less male than it once was.

Most parties have made substantial efforts to recruit candidates reflective of society. Some, like the NDP, have instituted specific nomination procedures to increase the number of women candidates (Young 1997b). The Liberal Party under Jean Chrétien was not afraid simply to drop candidates into specific ridings, even over the opposition of local party members. There is often some difficulty in finding competitive seats for candidates high on a party's list of hopeful members. High turnover and retirement rates in Canada have helped somewhat, as it is often easier to recruit candidates to open seats rather than trying to dislodge a sitting member at the nomination stage.

There has also been a wholesale shift in the manner in which prime ministers deal with the problem of inclusion in cabinets. The political need to reach out to women, visible minorities, and ethnic groups has led prime ministers make strategic cabinet choices. Since the 1970s prime ministers have gone to great lengths to make their cabinets as inclusive, and representative, as possible given the men and women in their caucus. Gender, language, ethnicity, and region are added to talent in the list of cabinet criteria.

Many of the problems surrounding inclusiveness are problems of representation. Numeric representation is how closely Parliament resembles the demographic profile of the country. Equally if not more important is substantive representation, members of different ethnic groups bringing different opinions and views to office. Jerome Black's (2002b, 355-69) work on representation in the House of Commons suggests that increasing diversity in the House does have the potential to alter the substantive representation of ethnic Canadians. He argues that the numeric representation in the Commons may still be too minimal to see the full effects of substantive representation. While this is no doubt true, the ability of members to provide substantive representation is often a function of their ability to participate fully in their assigned roles and duties.

Participation

The question of participation asks what opportunities are available for members to undertake their responsibilities. A club may be inclusive in allowing anyone to join. But once in the club, can members engage in all its activities? If not, what are the roadblocks to full participation? Participation within a parliamentary setting means the ability to fully engage in the functions of parliament, defined in the next section as scrutiny, legislation, and representation.

By its very nature, parliamentary government allows different degrees of participation to different members. At one end of the spectrum sit independent members or members of a caucus without recognized party status. Denied the funding for caucus research and the regular right to raise questions, these MPs or MLAs face an uphill battle in providing the same kind of representation to Canadians as other members. At the other extreme, members of cabinet both sit in the party that forms the government and are the only members of the legislative assembly allowed to introduce legislation that will draw funds from government coffers. The ability to introduce these so-called money bills is perhaps the greatest, but not the only, participatory reward of cabinet. Cabinet ministers draw additional salaries, tend to have longer – and safer – political careers, and have the greatest facility to influence public policy (Docherty and White 1999). Most members of parliamentary assemblies in Canada find themselves somewhere between these two extremes.

When thinking of participation three key issues must be addressed: size, opportunity, and power. First, is an assembly large enough to perform properly the duties of the assembly? Are there enough members to allow opposition and backbench government members to do their jobs? Low public regard for politicians has allowed provincial governments to decrease the size of many assemblies, despite growing populations in the provinces. This means more work for members both outside the chamber (more constituents to represent) and inside the assembly (fewer members to scrutinize the government).

Second, are enough opportunities available for members to fulfill their responsibilities? Even if a legislature has enough members, without opportunities to scrutinize the government, discuss and fine-tune legislation, and represent constituents, members would not be properly participating in the full legislative process. Question periods, debates, committee hearings, and resources for individual members allow them to participate in scrutiny of government and the representation of specific and general interests.

Third, do the members have the power to properly perform their duties? Even though members are allowed to debate, suggest policy reforms, hear from witnesses, and write reports, their suggestions and recommendations should have some chance of working their way into actual legislation or programs. The limited ability of members to force a government to act (or react) is the cause of great frustration to many MPs (Docherty 1999). We often think of party discipline as the major problem stifling politicians in Canada, but of much greater concern are the institutional restrictions on members in other parts of their legislative life. Among other recommendations, this audit concludes that continued committee reform will provide members with the best opportunity for improved participation.

The problem of participation is real in Canadian legislatures. The talents of many good men and women are wasted, not because of a lack of initiative, but rather a lack of opportunity to use these talents. This audit will examine how the combination of numbers and a concentration of authority in cabinet limits the ability of members to fully participate in representing Canadians.

The Functions of Modern Legislatures in Canada

Before engaging in an audit that measures the performance of legislatures in Canada, the criteria upon which these assemblies will be judged must be understood and articulated. In simple terms, before we say a legislature is doing a good or a bad job, we must first understand what job it should be doing. This audit will examine three broad functions of parliaments, both federal and provincial: representation, scrutiny, and legislation (Bagehot 1961; Norton 1981; Franks 1987). We will not only discuss the duties that parliaments traditionally have performed but will also recognize duties under these functions that parliaments *should* be performing – that citizens expect of them – even if some institutional renewal and reform would be required, including more use of committees to initiate legislation and allowing members to serve as delegates to their voters.

It is worth noting that when we discuss parliaments and legislative bodies, we are really talking about the collective roles of a group of individuals. The men and women elected (or in the case of the Canadian Senate, selected) to a legislature have duties as representatives. Collectively these duties become the functions of the legislature. Our traditional reliance on strong party discipline means that we tend to think of these as group functions and responsibilities. Nonetheless, acts of representation, scrutiny, and legislation all have both collective (party) and individual (member) components.

REPRESENTATION

Anthony Birch (1964, 12-17) identifies three major forms of representation: the representative as agent, the representative as elected official, and the representative as a person reflective of a specific cohort of the population. Typically in modern democracies we assume the second form of representation to be of primary importance. The validity of officials can be called into question if representatives are not elected. This is perhaps the greatest problem facing the Canadian Senate today. It is not elected and there is no venue for public input into the appointment process (Docherty 2002b, 170).

Of course, most Canadians want their elected members to act as agents of local concerns. Indeed, the concept of agent is the very foundation of voter anger at politicians who are seen to listen to the party and party leaders and not their local voters. We hope that our assemblies somehow reflect the face of the society they represent, though this ideal is rarely achieved.

In his now famous speech to the electors of Bristol in 1774 after his victory, Edmund Burke advised his constituents that a true representative owes voters "not his industry only but his judgement" (Burke 1834, 176-80). In voicing his support for legislators who place the natural or common good ahead of local concerns, Burke was dooming his chances of future re-election, at least in Bristol. But he was describing a form of representation that finds more favour in capitals than in constituencies. This historic speech, which contrasted two forms of representation – serving as the voice of a riding versus using wisdom to act for the common good – is as relevant in present-day debates on representation as it was over 200 years ago.

Birch is far from alone in his studies of representational styles and approaches. In the US context Heinz Eulau discussed three styles of representation: trustee, delegate, and politico (this last being a blend of the first two and therefore less relevant to the Canadian experience). Ironically, this work was done almost forty years ago, and even then there was a so-called "crisis of representation" (1978, 31). Although Eulau was not looking at the Canadian Parliament, when we talk about a democratic deficit, his analysis of trustees versus delegates remains informative for our analysis.

Trustees are just that: individuals in whom voters place a great deal of trust. Under this style voters assume that they are electing an individual who will use experience, wisdom, and foresight to rule in the best interest of broader community. For trustees, local interests are second to national concerns (Pitkin 1967). A trustee is almost a Burkean representative, unafraid to vote against local wishes if there is a more pressing common good. Of course in modern democracies, a politician who sticks too closely to a trustee style runs the risk of angering local voters who think that their member has lost touch with the views and needs of the riding.

Delegates have no time for a trustee style of representation. Delegates view themselves as the voice of their people, or at least the voice of the majority of their citizens. For delegates, notions of national interest take a distant back seat to local concerns. If one aggregates all local interests in all constituencies, a national interest will emerge. This delegate style tends to find a stronger home in the United States, where congressional government fosters a strong attachment to local concerns. Members of Congress are largely viewed as protectors of their districts. Delegate style might almost be seen as second best to direct democracy, which is impractical in large modern societies.

In the absence of a system that allows all citizens to vote on every issue, elected representatives are expected to protect and act as spokespeople for their constituencies (Docherty 2002b, 172-3). The key strength of a delegate is presumably his or her ability to be in constant touch with the needs of voters. Surveys suggest that over two-thirds of Canadians believe that politicians very quickly "lose touch with people" after an election (Howe and Northrup 2000, 9). This notion suggests that some representatives promise a particular style of representation when seeking office (presumably delegate), then switch to a very different approach once safely elected.

Delegate-style representation was certainly not what Burke originally believed was compatible with Westminster systems. In Westminster parliaments, in which the executive and the legislature sit together, party discipline is a requirement, at least for the governing party. It is also helpful for the opposition, which must stick together if it hopes to put forth a cohesive alternative platform. That is not to say that Canada has been without political parties that have put forth a delegate style of representation as a new approach to governing. In the early 1920s the Progressive Party tapped into alienation from Ottawa, particularly in the West. It found success with its grassroots approach. Among other reforms, it supported recall of sitting members, more national referenda, and more free votes and less party discipline (see Morton 1967). Ironically, this last position cost it dearly. In the 1921 general election, it actually came in second to the victorious Liberals. Yet the members refused to sit and serve as a unified party, effectively abdicating their role as the official opposition. Internal dissension within the party caused an irreconcilable split and it never recovered politically.

In terms of a grassroots, delegate-style approach, the most recent equivalent of the Progressive Party has been the Canadian Alliance (formerly the Reform Party), now merged into the Conservative Party of Canada. As a grassroots party, the Reform/Alliance had mixed success in sticking to delegate-style representation. Perhaps learning from the Progressive Party experience, many Reform/Alliance members of Parliament came to appreciate the benefits of solidarity within the party. If an opposition party wishes to oppose the government effectively, it must demonstrate some unity. If it does not, it is fair game for a prime minister and cabinet that paint it as unable to put forth an effective alternative government. Such a delegate style might win support at home, but gets nowhere in the capital.

Yet long before the Reform/Alliance success, members were trying to release themselves from the so-called shackles of party discipline in many innovative ways, whether through more effective use of private members' business or through reform of the committee system. Veteran legislators from the traditional parties understand that too much party discipline is harmful. It effectively limits meaningful participation from the majority of the assembly. At the same time, if there were no party discipline governments would have no capacity to respond to the collective good. The trick is in finding a balance that allows for effective responsiveness and meaningful participation. The Audit will examine representation in the sense of how members represent constituents and also interests that transcend the boundaries of individual ridings.

SCRUTINY

One of the most critical functions of members of Parliament is to act as a watchdog on the government of the day. Passive observers of parliamentary institutions who see that the executive sits as part of the legislative body can be forgiven for thinking of the government and Parliament as one body. Yet the differences are vast between the executive, which runs the government, and the legislature as a whole, which allows the government to operate and holds the executive to account.

The legislature keeps the government honest, because the government is accountable to the legislature. Members of the legislature who are not in cabinet are charged with ensuring that the government acts properly, spends wisely, and meets the needs of citizens. Scrutiny is the second half of government accountability in a Westminster system. The first half consists in the responsibility of ministers of the Crown for the actions of their departments' civil servants. Ministers must answer for these actions (or in some cases inaction) in the House of Commons. Members of Parliament are responsible to the people of Canada for ensuring that ministers account for themselves and their civil servants (see Docherty 1999). This accountability is exacted both by opposition members and by members of the governing party who are not in cabinet, that is, government backbenchers. Nationally, the Senate can also play an effective scrutiny role by holding up or tweaking legislation that is sent from the lower chamber.

Members have many vehicles at their disposal for holding government to account, some of which are based on the dominant party system and others predicated on the individual talents of members. Question period, debates on the budget and throne speech, the committee system, and caucus are among the most common. Depending on the time, the issue, and the players, opposition members choose the route that is most likely to make the government look bad and the opposition look good. Government backbenchers traditionally use the quieter, more secretive vehicle of caucus. Members also have the opportunity to perform this function via debates and voting on specific pieces of legislation; the legislative function is addressed separately below given its importance, particularly in terms of opportunities for renewal and reform.

Question period is undoubtedly the most popular and open forum for scrutiny of the government. Question periods vary by jurisdiction, but each elected assembly in Canada has one. It is the most watched activity when the House is sitting, and the part of the daily proceedings best attended by both members of Parliament and members of the press. Question period is popular among the opposition and press for one reason: it is the only time members of the executive (cabinet) are placed on the hot seat facing the opposition. It is also uniquely parliamentary: the US Congressional system does not have an equivalent to our question period. The president may have to answer a special prosecutor on occasion, but he or she will never have to face the entire Congress to answer their questions on policy issues or executive decisions. And unlike Great Britain, where most questions are presented to the minister prior to question time, question period in Canada is unscripted.

There are risks associated with question period for members of the opposition. The maxim "only ask a question you already know the answer to" is particularly true of question period queries. This error is most frequently made by rookie opposition MPs asking questions of experienced cabinet ministers. Instead of promoting scrutiny and accountability, opposition MPs inadvertently provide the government with an additional forum to boast of their accomplishments. A potentially more damaging drawback of question period is the rather raucous behaviour it encourages among members. Question period brings out the best in political theatre. At its finest, it showcases quick wit, sharp arguments, and the ability to down a political opponent armed only with detailed policy information and a fine debating skill. All too often, however, question period can resemble the lead-up to a wrestling match, with opponents slanging each other, oblivious to the policy points they should be arguing and the scrutiny function they should be performing. Parliaments must work hard to clean up these negative aspects of question period.

A second important opportunity for scrutiny is provided by the debates on the budget and speech from the throne. Members can hold the government to account on its major economic and social policies. At the same time, these debates allow members to address many local issues and concerns, and opposition members can lay out their own parties' political agendas. When times are good, the budget and speech from the throne are largely vehicles for the government to trumpet its message. When economic times are less certain, budget and throne speech debates can have a considerably different tone and knock a government off its set agenda.

Caucus as a method of scrutiny is available only to government back-benchers. While all political parties caucus, opposition parties use this time for strategic planning against the government (how best to carry out their scrutiny function and embarrass the government). Government caucus serves the scrutiny function more directly, because it operates under a thick shield of secrecy. Theoretically, secrecy allows all members to speak frankly and criticize ministers of the Crown, yet remain united once they face the public (and the opposition). In addition, cabinet ministers can float ideas past their peers knowing that they can be shot down without the government appearing weak.

Finally, the committee system provides some opportunities for scrutiny of government activity. Indeed, the biggest threat to committees is their inability to participate fully in the scrutiny function. For example, legislators express great frustration at the government estimates process. During estimates, committees examine the budgets, goals, and programs of various government departments. As legislative watchdogs, they are charged with ensuring that government departments are achieving their objectives as efficiently as possible. As elected representatives, members should also be in a position to make at least limited changes to the goals and directions of government departments. But they are prevented from making even modest changes within government spending lines. The net result is limited participation. Members may scrutinize but not initiate policy changes. If members had more power they could more actively respond to the demand for changes to spending priorities.

This type of problem frustrates private members and allows the public to see these individuals as less than productive. Scrutiny of government operations is a primary function of legislatures in Canada. Yet its success is mixed at best. The scrutiny opportunities that are conducive to embarrassing the government (and often to embarrassing Parliament as an institution) are those that are carried out most effectively by opposition members. Few scrutiny functions that are transparent to the public provide both effective participation by members and good governance. Not surprisingly, citizens question the value of representation that is not seen to be effective.

LEGISLATION

Westminster parliaments do not initiate legislation; rather they pass or defeat legislation that originates with the cabinet (Franks 1987). Further, the tendency of Canadian elections, both national and provincial, to produce majority governments means that most legislation will pass or die on the order paper as the government, not the legislature, sees fit. Nonetheless, legislation is a priority function of Parliament and parliamentarians, for three reasons.

First, Parliament is the one forum where open public debate *must* be held on legislation. There are no binding requirements on governments to hold prelegislative hearings, nor are governments required to hear from the public once a piece of legislation is introduced. But before any legislation can become law, there must be three readings and two sessions of debate on it. Moreover, because legislation is often sent to a committee for further study, opposition parties have at least two and sometimes three opportunities to debate legislation and provide the public with an accounting of government plans. The government also has at least two opportunities to explain its actions to the public.

Some legislation is of a housekeeping nature and does not generate significant media or public attention. But often legislation is contentious, and occasionally it does not have strong public support. In such cases, the opposition parties use their skills and parliamentary expertise to hinder the passage of a bill while trying to garner public support for their position. With a majority government, opposition parties are fully aware that the government will eventually win the day. But they can nonetheless embarrass the government and make it appear as if the government has little regard for voters.

One method at the government's disposal to limit embarrassment is to limit the amount of debate on legislation. Time allocation, which essentially limits the time to be spent debating a bill, is seen by the opposition as an affront to democratic representation and by the government as effective time management. While it may be true that the outcome of most votes are known in advance and endless debate can quickly become repetitive, the evidence at the federal level seems to be on the side of the opposition.

Second, although legislation is introduced by the government, it is altered through the legislature. In addition, the legislative process can provide an opportunity to include the public in policy debates. Committees of Parliament can play an extremely important role as legislation makes its way through the chamber. This role is twofold. First, committees can go through the often tedious, but always necessary, clause-by-clause debate of bills and offer numerous amendments to bills that might have been introduced too quickly and sloppily. Second, committees can call witnesses and have public hearings to allow further debate on an issue. Committees thus allow the government and opposition parties to reach out to their respective constituencies. Particularly with bills of a technical nature, committee hearings involve the testimony of expert witnesses. Here the process is educational, enabling members to learn on the job and become informed about the real implications of policy proposals.

In some cases, legislators are genuinely trying to understand the public's mood on an issue. But in other cases legislators understand public sentiment and use the committee stage simply as a way of gaining publicity and furthering their support among various groups. Often, committee hearings simply allow the government to explain its policy and legislative plans and try to make the unpalatable at least bearable. Jon Malloy's work (1996, 323-4) on the role of parliamentary committees during the GST debate suggests that this legitimating function was the only purpose of the public hearings. Committees serve an important role in communicating with the public.

Third, passage through the House of Commons and Senate, or provincial assemblies, is an important symbol that the laws and policies that derive from the bill are legitimate. The fact that a democratically elected legislature debated a bill and a majority of members voted in favour of it signifies that the law is valid. While this seems almost too obvious, it is an integral aspect of the legislative process. Bills cannot be given royal assent (marking their passage from the legislative stage into law) until they have passed third reading.

The questions a democratic audit must ask about the legislative function are readily identifiable. First, do members have the information and resources necessary to properly debate bills? Second, is there sufficient time available for this debate? Third, is there adequate opportunity for public input? Fourth, are members stretched too thin to properly participate at the committee stage of legislation? And most important, what remedies are available to offset deficiencies in any of these areas?

Outline of Audit

This volume examines the level of democratic participation available to members of legislative assemblies in Canada. It examines how legislative assemblies, never truly reflective of society, have nonetheless become more inclusive, through both the recruitment of candidates and improved local representation. It also examines how members are increasingly resisting party discipline and the potential challenges this poses to a government's ability to be responsive to citizens.

Where possible, provincial and territorial legislatures are included in the analysis, though the starting point for each examination remains the Canadian Parliament. However, this audit is neither exhaustive nor technical. There are many aspects of legislatures that we have not undertaken to examine. For example, when we examine how members allocate staff, we have not adopted a standard technique employed in accounting audits called "value for money." We do not comment on more appropriate ways to allocate staff, but rather comment on the ability of members to properly perform their functions using the resources they are given.

The Audit is helped by a series of unpublished surveys of members of the House of Commons and of members of provincial assemblies. The federal survey was conducted in 2001 and the survey of MLAs was undertaken in the spring of 2002. The response rate for the survey of MPs was 32.8 percent (98 of 298). Not including cabinet ministers the return rate was higher, at 35 percent. Such a response rate for a mail-back survey of members of Parliament is not out of line (see Docherty 1997). The returns were representative of broadly defined regional seat distributions (the West, Ontario, Quebec, eastern Canada), and thus generalizations on this basis are possible. The response rate in the survey of MLAs was lower, at just over 28 percent. While there were returns from each province, Quebec's were lower than they should have been on a proportional basis. In addition, many individuals did not identify their province. Nonetheless, with the exception of Quebec, we are comfortable making generalizations on a regional basis.

This Audit and Graham White's volume (2005) in this series make use of a 2002 survey of clerks of the provincial and territorial legislatures. While Westminster parliaments share many features, their written and unwritten rules can differ greatly. It is difficult to reduce practices to one or two words in a table. Therefore, the tables and accompanying explanations that make use of these data do so recognizing that they are not static and do not tell the entire story of each legislature's procedures.

It is worth noting that different provincial assemblies use different terms for members. In Ontario, legislators are called members of provincial parliament (MPPs). In Quebec they are members of the national assembly (MNAs), and in Newfoundland and Labrador they are members of the house of assembly (MHAs). For the purposes of simplicity and clarity provincial members in general will be referred to as MLAs, members of the legislative assembly, which is the most common term used in the provinces and territories.

This volume examines the functions of modern legislatures in Canada in terms of the Democratic Audit benchmarks of inclusiveness, participation, and responsiveness. Chapter 2 begins the discussion of representation by looking at the inclusiveness of Canadian legislatures. Inclusiveness and representation are interwoven: inclusive legislatures are better able to properly represent all citizens. Canadian legislatures today are not as monochrome as in previous generations. At the same time, legislatures are hardly a reflection of the society they represent.

Chapter 3 examines the functions of representation in terms of participation in assemblies, specifically, the positions of authority in the

Commons. Are members selected for cabinet based on notions of equity, fairness, and talent, or does loyalty to the leader trump these more noble criteria? Chapter 3 argues that most positions in the chamber – even outside of cabinet – help foster loyalty toward the party leader. The result is reinforcement of party discipline. Arguably, representation suffers as a result. Outside the legislature, members pursue the representation of citizens in a less partisan way. As Chapter 4 illustrates, members are good constituency representatives who work hard at individual casework. They do so in part out of dedication, but also because most assemblies provide elected representatives with the resources necessary to be responsive to citizens' needs.

After investigating representation in terms of the three benchmarks, we turn to the ability of members to properly engage in scrutiny. Chapter 5 looks at the participatory opportunities for scrutiny provided to members within legislatures, while Chapter 6 examines the problem of size in Canadian assemblies. Though the workload for members has not decreased since 1990, the number of men and women doing the job has gone down in five provinces. The problem of decreased legislative size has been exacerbated by an increase in cabinet size in many of the same jurisdictions. A larger workload for fewer members can create problems for responsiveness.

Ultimately, legislatures must legislate. Chapter 7 examines the process of government legislation from introduction through to defeat or passage. Chapter 7 also examines the role of the committee system in legislatures and how – if used properly – it can overcome an institutionalized barrier to broader public participation in a legislative assembly. In some small way this can overcome a lack of inclusiveness in the membership of a legislature. It definitely improves responsiveness.

Finally, this volume includes recommendations. Based on the analysis in the body of the book, Chapter 8 discusses recommendations for legislative reform in Canada, including both directions that legislatures might want to investigate, and paths that parliaments in Canada might best avoid. Specifically, this audit argues that the problem in Canadian representative assemblies is largely one of resources and rules. The lack of available resources limits the ability of members to properly represent their constituents inside the legislative environment. The overemphasis on party discipline and an obsession with the formal interpretation of confidence has limited the ability of all members, on both the opposition and government sides of the chamber, from proffering innovative debate and discussion. However, the answer is not simply to move in the direction of a congressional system (best exemplified by the US model), where party discipline is weaker but members are dependent instead on large fundraising interests. Instead, the concluding chapter argues that increasing the size of assemblies (thereby creating smaller, more homogenous constituencies) and increasing resources to members can go a long way to redressing the problem of strong parties without diluting the strength of representation provided by our Westminster-style assemblies.

Chapter 1

Strengths

- Legislatures lie at the centre of Canadian democracy. They are the only popularly selected representatives of the people.

- The primary functions of modern legislatures are representation, scrutiny, and legislation.

- Representation includes voicing concerns of those inside and outside an elected member's riding.

- Scrutiny entails keeping the government accountable for its actions.

- Legislation focuses on passing, fine-tuning, or defeating government-initiated bills and policies.

Weaknesses

- Party discipline can prevent members from voting as they think best.

- By their nature, legislatures limit most participation to those fortunate enough to be elected.

- Both formal and informal rules of legislatures limit the ability of some members to participate fully in their legislative and scrutiny functions.

2 WHO REPRESENTS CANADIANS?

This chapter focuses on the question of how reflective Canadian assemblies are of the society they represent. This type of representation has close links to the Audit benchmark of inclusiveness. Understanding if and how a legislature includes (or excludes) certain segments of society is an important starting point. A legislature whose membership includes many of the diverse communities that constitute the Canadian cultural mosaic is probably in a much better position to respond effectively to the problems faced by particular communities within our society. This chapter examines how closely legislatures in Canada reflect the population they represent, in terms of gender, ethnic background, and occupation.

Part of the problem with such an inquiry is determining what a perfect assembly would look like. We can imagine an ideal assembly that completely mirrors our society: the same proportion of men and women, linguistic diversity, visible minorities, all religions — an exact replica of Canada at this very moment. Realizing that ideal raises two questions: how big and unwieldy would such an assembly be, and how can it be created within a democratic context where citizens are free to vote for (and against) any candidate they wish? Therefore this chapter does not create an ideal legislature and hold Canada's assemblies up to such a hypothetical standard. Instead it concentrates on how the makeup of legislatures has developed over the past sixty years. The formal rules that govern who can run and sit in Canadian legislatures exclude few citizens, but informal barriers to participation and inclusiveness remain. Canadian assemblies are more representative of Canadian society today than previously, but we still need more women and visible minorities in positions of power, for we are still a long way from truly representative assemblies.

Representation and Inclusiveness

Representation lies at the heart not just of legislatures but of modern democracies. Nothing is more central to democracy than the premise that citizens have a voice in the governing of their society. The size and population of modern democracies require that they be indirect, or representative. Citizens look to their elected (or appointed, as in the case of the Canadian Senate) officials to "represent" their interests in their national or provincial capital.

Representation encompasses a wide range of styles and approaches. As discussed in Chapter 1, Anthony Birch's (1964, 12-17) three types of representation – agent, elected official, and someone who represents a specific group in society – all have validity in the Canadian context. These are far from mutually exclusive types. An agent acts much like a solicitor, representing someone's interests even if that means going against that individual's short-term desires. An elected official acts to please those that sent him or her off to office. The third type suggests some form of mirror representation wherein a group within society needs someone from within it to represent it in a larger body.

In indirect democracies, one representative commonly serves as all three types simultaneously. MPs, for example, act on behalf of their constituents. Where possible, they try to act in accordance with the views of the majority of their voters, though their actions will always displease some. However, MPs believe that they are acting in the long-term interests of the larger community.

Within the riding, members see their duty as speaking and acting on behalf of constituents. The duty may be specific to individuals, as in such classic constituency casework as immigration or employment insurance assistance. It may be aimed at groups in the riding – helping a volunteer group receive funding for a local project. Or it might encompass broader representation – letting the government know what the good burghers of constituency X think about an issue. In each of these cases members are seen as the voice and hands of the region. Some of this work takes place in the riding and some in Ottawa.

We can broaden the representation function further to include representing interests outside a member's individual constituency. Members represent their own voters, but they are also expected to represent like-minded individuals across the country. In part this expectation simply stems from their official duties in the House. Cabinet ministers wear two hats: a minister in charge of a particular department is simultaneously a member who represents particular individuals within a specified geographic territory. Critics, or shadow cabinet ministers, do likewise. Thus, a critic for veterans' affairs speaks not just for his or her constituents but also represents all Canadian war veterans. In addition, members may also speak on behalf of Canadians who share their demographic characteristics (Docherty 2002c). Female MPs are seen to represent Canadian women, for example, and Aboriginal MPs are expected to protect the interests of Native Canadians. Often members do not particularly relish this additional role, and some openly reject it. In other cases it is welcomed and sought out.

The important point is that the latter two types of representation easily transcend a particular geographically defined constituency. Further, while this type of activity may be categorized as policy or partisan work, it is a representative function of members, and is undertaken at least partially to respond to demands of Canadians and segments of the population. Group representation is as crucial as agent or delegate representation. Furthermore, if done effectively, it allows members to make up for a lack of inclusiveness, or mirror representation, inside the legislative chamber. An elected official may look like and share the first language of a majority of his or her voters, but one person cannot reflect the entire citizenry of a single-member district. Even in smaller districts, such as the twenty-seven provincial seats in Prince Edward

Island, mirror representation is impossible at the individual riding level. Speaking on behalf of individuals or underrepresented groups outside one's constituency ameliorates this deficiency.

Such representation, however, is possible only if a legislature as a whole reflects to some extent the population of its jurisdiction. How closely do Canadian legislatures reflect the broader population? Do all Canadians have an equal opportunity to participate as elected representatives?

Formal Barriers to Participation

Few formal barriers to participation in public office exist in Canada. With few exceptions, most Canadians are eligible to run for office in the provinces and federally. This has not always been the case, and our legislatures are certainly more open now than they were even fifty years ago. A combination of electoral reforms and court decisions has opened up the process in the past two decades.

The age requirement for voting and serving in public office is consistent across the country, at eighteen. For the most part, anyone eligible to vote has also been seen as fit to serve. Once granted the franchise, individuals were free to compete for the opportunity to fully participate in legislative proceedings. In some cases, however, the removal of the final formal barrier to participation was not concomitant with the right to vote. In many jurisdictions, women were denied the ability to serve until a year or two after being granted the right to vote. This goes beyond the delay between new legislation and the next election: in New Brunswick, the delay was almost fifteen years (Bashevkin 1985, 6).

Further, those shut out of the process have not always agreed that being let in is a good thing. Participation in the electoral process can come at too high a cost. As recently as the 1950s, the cost of electoral participation for many Aboriginals was the formal renouncement of their group and individual identity. Under these conditions it was hardly surprising that few Aboriginals chose to vote (Royal Commission on Aboriginal Peoples 1996, 287).

Changes to federal electoral laws in the early 1990s made it possible for those with developmental challenges to participate in the electoral system. By 1993 the only adult Canadian citizens not allowed to vote federally were individuals serving more than a two-year prison sentence. A Supreme Court of Canada decision found that law unconstitutional (*Sauvé* v. *Canada* 2002; also Courtney 2004, 36-8). This removed the last of the formal barriers to participation in voting. These historical barriers to voting serve as reminders that democratic representation and participation are fluid and evolving. We may see ourselves as truly open, but a quick look at our history suggests that we are continuing on a path of greater participation and inclusiveness, which has yet to be fully travelled.

The only legislative chamber in Canada that has not removed the primary legislative barriers to service is the Senate. The sole remaining upper chamber in Canada, the Senate was created to be a voice for regional and propertied interests. The criteria for Senate eligibility, as delineated in the Constitution, reflect these goals by ensuring regional representation. In 1867 the Senate had seventy-two members, twenty-four for each of Ontario, Quebec, and the Maritime provinces (Nova Scotia and New Brunswick). Today, Ontario and Quebec are still considered regions unto themselves with twenty-four seats each. The West (Alberta, British Columbia, Saskatchewan, and Manitoba) has twenty-four seats, as do the Maritimes (New Brunswick, Nova Scotia, and Prince Edward Island). Newfoundland and Labrador has six seats, and each territory has one.

Beside regional representation, there are two other criteria for appointment that reflect the original view of the Canadian Senate as a chamber of sober reflection: age and property. Section 23 of the Constitution Act 1867 sets the age necessary to enter the Senate at thirty. The age requirement underscores that senators were intended to have some external experience prior to sitting in the Senate, and thus presumably to have a greater and more contemplative world view. The property requirement of $4,000 was far less controversial in 1867 than the distribution of seats. At that time, owning property was an essential qualification for any Canadian seeking federal public office (MacKay 1963, 45-7). Today, the property qualification is more of an anachronism than a barrier to appointment. The fact that it remains in place is largely due to prime ministers' fear of inviting a discussion of Senate reform that requires constitutional change (Docherty 2002a, 29-30).

Informal Barriers to Participation

It might be difficult to believe, but Canada's first federal Jewish cabinet minister was a member of cabinet until 2002. Though this says almost as much about Herb Gray's longevity as it does about past unwillingness to have a more diverse cabinet, it speaks to the relatively recent change in the approach of prime ministers when it comes to selecting ministers from the government caucus. At one time, members of religious, ethnic, or visible minorities were consciously left out of the highest levels of government. Today they are consciously recruited to run for office.

Informal barriers to participation can occur at many stages. First, party members might decline to nominate particular types of Canadians. Second, voters might decide not to elect them. Third, party leaders might decide not to allow successful candidates to occupy positions of authority within the caucus or cabinet. The first two stages are beyond the scope of this particular audit. As Bill Cross (2004) demonstrates in his volume in this series, some parties have used the nomination process to increase the number of female candidates, while others have allowed the local constituencies to determine their candidates. In the 1993 and 1997 elections, Jean Chrétien used his leader prerogative to place high-profile candidates (most of them female) in ridings the Liberal Party had a very good chance of capturing. The nomination process has historically been the largest barrier to increased gender representation in Canadian assemblies (Young 1991).

Certainly in districts where a party is not seen as competitive, it is easier for anyone, regardless of gender or ethnicity, to gain a nomination

– no one else wants it. But once nominated, there is no guarantee that a candidate will overcome the second potential barrier. Determining resistance at the polls based on the demographic characteristics of candidates is difficult at the best of times. Even with election study data, determining levels of prejudice or resistance to change is futile.

However, we can examine both occupational and demographic profiles of members of various assemblies over time to determine whether legislatures are becoming more representative of the people they serve. This inquiry is admittedly second best. It does not tell us whether members of various minorities failed to get nominated or elected, nor does it illuminate the root causes of nonrepresentation. Nonetheless, it does help us determine whether Canadian legislatures are moving in the right direction.

Gender Representation in Canadian Legislatures

Were assemblies in Canada more reflective of the population in 2001 than they were in 1971 or 1941? The quick answer is yes, but a great deal of improvement is still necessary. As Table 2.1 demonstrates, women have made substantial progress in terms of representation. By 1941 all Canadian women were allowed to vote and sit in assemblies. Nevertheless, women were far from common in the Commons, or in any other legislature for that matter. Nationally, Dorise Neilsen from Saskatchewan was the only woman in the House, though Agnes Macphail from Ontario served from 1921 until defeated in 1940. The majority of provincial assemblies were still all-male in 1941.

Thirty years later, although the second wave of feminism was in full swing and achieving success in some fields, most legislatures were at least 90 percent male. Only in British Columbia did men make up less than nine in ten MLAs. As Sylvia Bashevkin (1985) has argued eloquently, although gender was on the political agenda, the political landscape was hardly equitable. Women were still relegated to the less glamorous realm of local partisan organizing, and were not involved in policy discussions or engaged in democratic representation.

Table 2.1

Gender representation in Canadian legislatures, 1941, 1971, 2001

Jurisdiction	1941 (%)		1971 (%)		2001 (%)	
	Legislature	Population	Legislature	Population	Legislature	Population
House of Commons						
Male	99.6	51.3	97.7	51.1	80.1	49.5
Female	0.4	48.7	2.3	48.9	19.9	50.5
Senate						
Male	96.8	51.3	92.6	51.1	66.3	49.5
Female	3.2	48.7	7.4	48.9	33.7	50.5
Newfoundland						
Male	n/a		100.0	51.0	83.3	49.5
Female			0.0	49.0	16.7	50.5
Prince Edward Island						
Male	100.0	51.8	100.0	50.4	81.5	49.0
Female	0.0	48.2	0.0	49.6	18.5	51.0
Nova Scotia						
Male	100.0	51.2	100.0	50.3	90.4	49.0
Female	0.0	48.8	0.0	49.7	9.6	51.0
New Brunswick						
Male	93.6	51.2	98.2	50.3	80.4	49.5
Female	0.0	48.8	1.8	49.7	19.6	50.5
Not given	6.4					
Quebec						
Male	98.8	52.2	98.8	49.7	76.0	49.3
Female	0.0	47.8	0.9	50.3	24.0	50.7
Not given	1.2		0.9			
Ontario						
Male	98.8	57.7	98.3	49.9	81.6	49.3
Female	1.2	42.3	1.7	50.1	18.4	50.4
Manitoba						
Male	96.3	51.8	94.6	50.0	76.4	49.6
Female	3.7	48.2	1.8	50.0	23.6	50.4
Not given			3.6			
Saskatchewan						
Male	100.0	51.7	100.0	50.8	77.2	49.6
Female	0.0	48.3	0.0	49.2	22.8	50.4
Alberta						
Male	98.2	53.7	96.0	50.9	72.3	50.5
Female	1.8	46.3	4.0	49.1	27.7	49.5
British Columbia						
Male	93.8	53.2	89.1	50.4	70.7	49.6
Female	6.2	46.8	10.9	49.6	29.3	50.4

Note: Newfoundland was not part of Canada in 1941 and was governed by a commission.
Source: Statistics Canada 1973; 2002.

It is worth noting that equality in gender representation has been as much of a struggle provincially as nationally, despite the fact that provincial governments have more direct responsibility over such social policy fields as health and education. These areas are often referred to as "women's issues," not because they affect only women, but because women are more likely than men to feel the impact of policy changes in these fields. Further, there is strong evidence that women are much more likely than men to base their choice about how to vote upon a political party's stance on education, health, or other "social policy" issues (Everitt 2002, 110-14).

The thirty years after 1971 saw more rapid change, but only when judged against the snail's pace of the previous three decades. A year into the new millennium, at least one-fifth of all members were female in half of the assemblies in Canada. In all but one assembly, the proportion of women was over 10 percent. Again, this is hardly cause for celebration.

One note of caution about Table 2.1: although data presented over time allow changes to be observed, the thirty-year gaps mean that some important data are missing. The three sample years were chosen to demonstrate changes over sixty years in a quick but meaningful way, and by and large the table does reflect the reality of each assembly during the time in question. However, some important trends emerged during the periods not shown. For example, in Table 2.1 it appears as if no women were elected in Prince Edward Island until the end of the twentieth century. As it turns out, PEI had a better gender-equity record than many provinces during the 1970s and 1980s. In 1981 three of thirty-two MLAs in PEI were women, and in 1985 five MLAs were women (14 percent).

Why were there more women serving in PEI? At least part of the answer lies in the way seats were distributed in Prince Edward Island. Until 1996 every constituency in PEI was a "double seat" constituency; every riding elected two members to serve in the assembly. There were sixteen ridings and thus thirty-two MLAs. Each party ran two candidates per riding. Balancing gender – and other social factors – was easier under such a system. Indeed, gender was a distant second consideration behind religion in the province. The informal practice of the two main Island parties, the Liberals and Progressive Conservatives, was to run one Roman Catholic and one Protestant in each riding (Dyck 1996, 96). Even with the religious split, women in Prince Edward Island fared much better than in other provinces under such a system. In fact, the Canadian Advisory Council on the Status of Women recommended just such a system to the Royal Commission on Electoral Reform and Party Financing (1991, 44-5). While the Lortie Commission did not include double ridings in its recommendations, this system was given some consideration.

The notion of double ridings was taken very seriously by the people of Nunavut when constructing their new districts (Young 1997a). A referendum was held to determine if voters would institute double ridings expressly to ensure gender equality. It was defeated in May 1997. The mere fact that the idea was taken so seriously, however, stands as a strong reminder that the way ridings are constructed can have an important impact on inclusiveness and representation.

Although most elections in the 1980s and 1990s brought record numbers of women into legislatures, this is a product more of the dearth of women previously than of the achievement of gender-equal representation. Surpassing past achievements is not difficult when the achievements are dubious at best. Nonetheless, inclusiveness in terms of gender has increased in every jurisdiction. It should be noted that improvements in gender representation occasionally take place for less-than-positive reasons. For example, in the 1984 and 1993 federal general elections, women were not so much elected to office, as male incumbents were defeated. In 1980 the Progressive Conservatives had elected only two women, while ten female Liberal candidates were successful. When the Conservatives won their massive majority four years later, and the Liberals were swept from office, the two parties elected nineteen and five women respectively. Likewise, in 1993 when the Conservatives were swept from power and the Liberals returned to office, the number of successful female Grits nearly tripled from thirteen to thirty-six. In short, substantial increases in the proportion of women MPs occur during major government transitions.

The growth that occurs when governments are re-elected is far less dramatic.

Turnover at election time is the single largest opportunity Canadians have to elect new and potentially more diverse or representative men and women to office. If an election produces low turnover little new blood is brought into an institution. At the national level, Canada enjoys high levels of turnover (Docherty 1997). In most elections, at least one-third and sometimes well over half of the incumbents do not return. The largest single cause of turnover federally is electoral defeat as opposed to MPs deciding not to run for re-election (voluntary vacancy). Many provincial assemblies also have high levels of turnover from electoral defeat. Consecutive changing governments in Ontario between 1987 and 1995 meant increases and then decreases in gender equality. In Alberta, where the Progressive Conservative government has dominated without interruption or even serious threat since 1971, voluntary vacancy is the largest single determinant of turnover. This has meant fewer swings back and forth. Nonetheless Alberta's progress on gender equality is impressive, at least in relative terms. Since 1971 the Alberta legislative assembly has gone from just 4 percent women to over 27 percent.

ETHNORACIAL INCLUSIVENESS IN THE HOUSE OF COMMONS

Inclusiveness has been less successful in terms of the election of minorities to the federal Parliament. Jerome Black argues that after successive elections in which the number of ethnic minority MPs increased, the 2000 general election brought about an actual *decline* in the percentage of minority MPs (defined as non-British, non-French backgrounds). From a high of 24.95 percent of all members in 1997, the percentage of ethnoracial minorities dropped to 23.6 percent after the 2000 vote (see Table 2.2; Black 2002a, 25). Black argues that the drop, while admittedly not huge, is troubling since newly elected members represented the largest decrease. Ethnoracial incumbents held their own, but challengers were less successful. It is premature to speculate

Table 2.2

Ethnoracial origins of Canadian MPs, 1993-2000

Ethnoracial origin	1993 Number	1993 %	1997 Number	1997 %	2000 Number	2000 %
Majority	193	65.4	194	64.5	190	63.1
Majority-minority	27	9.2	24	8.0	34	11.3
Minority	71	24.1	75	24.9	71	23.6
European	53	18.0	52	17.3	49	16.3
Jewish	4	1.4	4	1.3	5	1.7
Visible minorities	13	4.4	19	6.3	17	5.6
Other	1	0.3				
Aboriginal	4	1.4	7	2.3	5	1.7
Other			1	0.3	1	0.3
Total	295		301		301	

Note: Column totals reflect that some members are counted in more than one category.
Source: Table reproduced in full, with permission, from Black 2002a.

on the cause for this. It may be tied to safe seats or it may be that ethnoracial minorities were less successful getting nominated in competitive ridings. Black's study does indicate that the overall trend in Canada is toward a more inclusive Parliament, one that comes closer to reflecting society than it did a generation ago. At the same time, he notes with concern that the increasing proportion of minority MPs is far lower than the increasing proportion of minority Canadians.

As Black suggests, minorities are not making huge strides in terms of inclusion in the Commons. Statistics Canada has indicated that just under 12 percent of Canadians are visible minorities (Black 2002b, 361). If this is the case then Parliament would have to double the number of visible minority MPs before matching the larger Canadian population.

It might be natural to assume that once elected, an MP from a visible minority would have an easier path to cabinet. What prime minister or premier would not want to reach out to one of Canada's multicultural communities by appointing a member of that community to a cabinet seat? There is some truth to this. In one of Jean Chrétien's cabinets, ministers such as Hedy Fry from British Columbia and Rey Pagtakhan from Manitoba might have been considered high-profile appointments, though their responsibilities (multiculturalism and veterans' affairs, respectively) were not considered senior cabinet seats. Ironically, shortly after Canada's first federal Jewish cabinet minister, Herb Gray, retired from office, the prime minister promoted the first woman of colour to the executive, Jean Augustine. This is not to suggest that the prime minister had an informal quota of ethnic or religious seats for cabinet, but that there is still a long climb ahead for members of visible minorities and other underrepresented groups in legislatures across the country.

Occupations in Assemblies

Assessing the representativeness of a legislative assembly in terms of occupations is more difficult. The diversity of occupations makes any significant comparisons extremely tenuous, particularly in the provinces. Further, in the interests of simplicity and drawing some reasonable generalizations, this study does not include an exhaustive study of occupational backgrounds in all legislatures over time. Few studies have looked at this, though as John Courtney (1974) has lamented this is partially due to the difficulty of finding modern data. Until 1972 the occupations of candidates for office were listed on the ballot. This provided a treasure trove of information on both lawmakers and those seeking office. Changes to the Canada Elections Act replaced occupation with party, which not only increased the role of party in the election process but decreased the name recognition of the local candidate. As Courtney argues, this was not necessarily a positive development (90).

Nonetheless, and once more acknowledging the shortcomings of thirty-year gaps in the data, looking at the occupations of legislators is a helpful exercise. As Table 2.3 indicates, some significant changes have taken place in every legislature in the country in the past six decades. The first point to note is the decrease in the number of farmers and fishers among elected representatives. This decrease corresponds to

Table 2.3

Occupational representation in Canadian legislatures, 1941, 1971, 2001

Jurisdiction	1941 (%)		1971 (%)		2001 (%)	
	Legislature	Population	Legislature	Population	Legislature	Population
House of Commons						
Farmers	17.1	14.5	6.5	2.7	4.9	2.2
Legal profession	31.4	0.2	25.3	0.2	12.7	0.5
Educators	5.3	2.1	10.4	4.0	18.4	6.4
Senate						
Farmers	10.9	14.5	5.4	2.7	0.7	2.2
Legal profession	33.2	0.2	31.6	0.2	7.9	0.5
Educators	0.0	2.1	7.5	4.0	5.1	6.4
Newfoundland and Labrador						
Farmers	n/a		2.2	0.2	2.0	0.7
Fishers			0.0	4.7	0.0	—
Legal profession			11.1	0.0	7.8	0.3
Educators			4.4	4.7	31.5	8.2
Prince Edward Island						
Farmers	16.5	29.5	13.9	6.5	13.3	5.4
Fishers	0.0	5.2	0.0	4.6	0.0	—
Legal profession	4.7	0.2	5.6	0.1	3.3	0.3
Educators	1.2	2.5	2.8	4.5	13.3	7.1
Nova Scotia						
Farmers	6.1	10.6	6.7	1.0	3.6	1.5
Fishers	0.0	5.3	2.0	2.0	0.0	—
Legal profession	21.2	0.2	24.5	0.2	13.7	0.5
Educators	0.0	2.0	8.2	4.4	21.7	7.8
New Brunswick						
Farmers	13.8	15.1	8.5	1.2	3.4	1.6
Fishers	0.0	2.8	0.0	1.0	0.0	—
Legal profession	15.7	0.2	16.7	0.2	10.2	0.4
Educators	2.0	2.1	10.0	4.4	17.0	6.9
Quebec						
Farmers	4.5	10.8	2.7	1.6	1.6	1.7
Legal profession	27.2	0.2	15.2	0.2	21.1	0.6
Educators	2.2	2.6	7.2	4.5	25.0	6.2
Ontario						
Farmers	22.4	10.3	8.4	1.6	1.9	1.4
Legal profession	19.1	0.2	14.3	0.3	16.9	0.5
Educators	1.1	1.5	7.4	3.8	14.9	6.0
Manitoba						
Farmers	18.9	18.9	18.4	6.1	12.0	5.6
Legal profession	13.8	0.2	8.3	0.2	5.2	0.3
Educators	8.6	1.9	10.1	3.9	22.4	7.1

Jurisdiction	1941 (%) Legislature	1941 (%) Population	1971 (%) Legislature	1971 (%) Population	2001 (%) Legislature	2001 (%) Population
Saskatchewan						
Farmers	41.1	36.9	33.0	16.0	20.1	9.9
Legal profession	14.3	0.1	4.7	0.1	6.7	0.4
Educators	1.8	2.4	16.7	4.0	6.7	7.2
Alberta						
Farmers	15.3	30.1	14.0	6.3	6.9	4.2
Legal profession	8.5	0.2	11.4	0.2	4.7	0.5
Educators	17.0	2.1	3.9	4.1	21.0	6.3
British Columbia						
Farmers	9.6	7.4	7.3	0.8	2.6	1.7
Fishers	0.0	2.3	1.7	0.4	0.0	—
Legal profession	11.5	0.2	11.9	0.3	10.3	0.5
Educators	1.9	1.6	8.5	3.5	16.7	7.0

Note: Newfoundland was not part of Canada in 1941 and was governed by a commission.
Sources: Canadian Parliamentary Guides, 1941, 1971, 2004; Dominion Bureau of Statistics 1946; Statistics Canada 1974, 2002.

the overall decrease in the population of these two groups. In defining farmers, fishers, and those in the education system and the legal profession, we employ the occupation classifications used by Statistics Canada in all three periods.

The percentage of farmers in legislatures has decreased substantially. The professionalization of most legislatures since the Second World War has meant that assemblies no longer meet only in late fall and early winter. This may have reduced the ability of some farmers to serve as MPs or MLAs. More important, by 2001 the actual number of farmers had decreased substantially across the country. Though farming was once the dominant source of income in Prince Edward Island, less than 6 percent of Islanders are now farmers. A similar drop can be found in every province. But the decrease in the proportion of farmers in legislatures over the past sixty years is less than the decrease in farmers in the population. Provinces with a heavy reliance on agriculture retain a strong critical mass of farmers in the legislature.

Despite the importance of the fishing industry to some provinces – namely PEI and Newfoundland and Labrador – it is far more likely to be underrepresented than farmers. In fact, fisher people have not done well when it comes to being elected. While farmers continue to be over-represented, many ocean provinces fail to send any fisher men or women to provincial office.

The conventional perception that the legal profession has a choke hold on assemblies is not without empirical support. In the years covered in Table 2.3, lawyers were not underrepresented in any provincial or federal assembly in Canada. In light of the consistent dominance of lawyers in legislative assemblies in Canada, the intervening years are unlikely to have deviated from this pattern. Is it harmful to have too many lawyers in a chamber? Given that one of the tasks of assemblies is to pass or defeat legislation, it may be helpful to have a jury of lawyers in an elected chamber. However, just as too many men in a Parliament might neglect a female perspective on issues, too many lawyers might be overly focused on legal concerns and ignore important economic, social, and political aspects of a piece of legislation.

Those concerned about the overrepresentation of lawyers can find some small comfort in that fact that their dominance is diminishing. In most jurisdictions, educators had replaced lawyers as the single dominant occupation group in 2001. The past sixty years have witnessed an extraordinary increase in the number of educators in provincial and federal legislatures. This trend in Canada follows other jurisdictions, such as the United Kingdom, where professionalization of politics has coincided with a change in the type of person elected to office and in particular a rise in the number of teachers and professors entering elected life (King 1981).

THE INCLUSIVE SENATE

Among the many complaints Canadians make about the Senate is that the appointed nature of this legislature allows prime ministers to select only partisan cronies as senators. It is often argued that the Senate is a vehicle for rewarding past partisan service, not a forum for debating the nation's business. As a result, one might be forgiven for thinking that the Senate is even less inclusive than the Commons.

Table 2.4

House of Commons and Senate: Characteristics of members, September 2000

Chamber	Age entered	Years served	Women (%)	Aboriginal (%)
House of Commons	50.8	6.3	20.9	1.7
Senate	63.3	9.7	33.3	5.0

Note: Years served does not include new members after 2000.
Sources: Docherty 2002a, tables 1 and 2.

After all, the appointment process allows prime ministers to bypass the electoral process. Is this the case? If our democratically elected chambers are not particularly inclusive, does our sole appointed body fare much better?

In terms of service, the Senate is a more experienced and tenured body than the Commons. As Table 2.4 indicates, senators tend to enter the Parliament at a later age and stay longer. Of course the fact that the average age of entry is sixty-three means less when we remember that these men and women do not have to retire until age seventy-five. The average senator will therefore serve for over twelve years before retirement. Trudeau and Mulroney appointees (who tended to be younger), will serve closer to twenty or more years. Prime Minister Chrétien's habit of appointing men and women in their early seventies did not help the reputation of the Senate as a patronage hall rather than a place of representative reflection. Indeed, of Chrétien's seventy-five appointments to the Senate, nineteen (or 25 percent) were at least seventy years old when they received the call. Of those nineteen, nine were at lease seventy-three years old at the time of their appointment.

Although the Senate is an unelected body, some senators hold a wide range of elected experience. There is little difference with regard to provincial political experience between members of the Commons (8.6 percent) and the Senate (11.6 percent). Although over one-fifth of all senators have experience as Commoners, very few Chrétien appointees fit this category. The result is a Senate of extremes. On one side are many long-serving senators, some of whom are career legislators and bring to the Senate a wealth of legislative wisdom. On the other side are men and women who are clearly in the Senate for a brief reward for a lifetime of partisan or public service. They will leave the Senate before they have fully learned the ropes. As a result, their ability to represent any interests effectively is questionable.

While neither the House nor the Senate comes close to reflecting the broader public, the appointed nature of the upper chamber allows the prime minister to make up for some of the shortfall in the House. Since women were allowed to sit in the Senate in 1930 it has had greater gender equality than the House of Commons. In 2000, one-third of all senators were women compared to one in five in the House. Prime ministers have also been aggressive in appointing Aboriginal senators: 5 percent of senators were Aboriginal in 2000, compared to less than 2 percent of members of Parliament.

Prime ministers can use the appointment process equally effectively to provide some form of representation based on occupational background, in exactly the same manner that they improve gender balance and Aboriginal representation. The business community is certainly overrepresented in the Senate, but less so than in the House of Commons. The Senate also exaggerates representation in areas that are typically thought of as being shut out of public office, namely arts and culture.

The representative function of the Senate has undergone some evolution. It no longer serves as a vehicle for strong regional representation, as this role has been taken by provincial premiers. The Senate is now rarely used to make up for a lack of provincial representation at the cabinet table. The ability of the governing party to win seats in every region in the past five elections has meant that prime ministers have not had to turn to this method of representation. It does remain as a safety net should a future government be less successful in every region.

The Senate does provide an arena for some underrepresented groups. It has been used by successive prime ministers to boost the number of female, minority, and Aboriginal parliamentarians, and to reward members of the artistic community as well. Nonetheless it remains largely a chamber of former lower house legislators and partisan loyalists. And as long as it remains such, its public image is unlikely to improve. This is unfortunate, for on many occasions the Senate has been forceful and produced thoughtful, alternative public policy visions (Docherty 2002a, 33).

Conclusion

This chapter has not attempted to set a standard for legislatures in terms of inclusiveness. We agree that individuals who share a characteristic of a group – be it gender, ethnicity, or religious affiliation – are better positioned to speak and act on behalf of that group than individuals who do not share similar traits (Black 2002b, 355). However, we do not suggest that mirror representation is a necessary or proper goal of assemblies.

It is difficult for a legislature to be truly inclusive in the sense of actually reflecting the population. With approximately one representative per 100,000 Canadians, obviously some elements of society are going to be left out. And while this leads to a form of systemic underrepresentation (some groups are more regularly left out than others), Canadian legislatures are becoming more representative of the population they serve. Formal barriers to election have all but been removed. Informal barriers are becoming smaller.

In some cases, political parties have made a more inclusive slate of candidates a priority; in other cases change has occurred more by happenstance. One of the more ironic – yet in many ways understandable – findings in this chapter is that the Senate is perhaps the most representative of all chambers. The unlimited power to appoint provides prime ministers the opportunity to reflect the Canadian population more accurately. Yet the Senate's more inclusive nature raises two points about legislative inclusiveness and representation.

First, when prime ministers use their Senate appointments to defend a record on gender or ethnoracial equity, they are also pointing to the deficiencies within their elected caucus. The January 2002 cabinet shuffle is a perfect illustration of this problem. As much as Prime Minister Chrétien tried to use appointed officials to prove his strong record on gender, MPs such as Carolyn Bennett could point to his lack of promotion of women to cabinet to paint a very different picture (Bennett 2002). Here Chrétien was doubly damned. Not only was there a smaller proportion of elected women than of appointed ones, but he had also failed to promote enough women in the former category to cabinet.

Second, a higher level of inclusiveness has hardly jumped the Senate to the head of the legitimacy list. Despite the efforts of senators such as Lowell Murray (2000) and Serge Joyal (2000), who have written on the positive aspects of the senior chamber, it remains a much maligned body. The root of the Senate's low public ratings may well have nothing to do with the actual appointments and more to do with the appointment process. Until senators are selected in a more transparent manner, the public will continue to view the upper chamber and its members critically, even those who make valuable contributions to representation and scrutiny. In other words, simply being more inclusive is not enough. A society may be perfectly reflected by the membership of its legislature. But if members are not permitted to participate fully, or if their efforts at participation are not rewarded with results, an inclusive assembly is hardly better than an exclusive club that represents only particular interests.

The next chapter examines responsiveness and participation within the legislature. Do legislatures provide opportunities to elected officials to participate fully in their representative functions? And if so, do elected members make up for a lack of inclusiveness and representation by speaking up for different groups? Or do members use opportunities within the legislature to reinforce partisan concerns?

Chapter 2

Strengths

- Most formal barriers to being elected have been eliminated, though many informal barriers remain.
- The number of lawyers in Canadian legislatures continues to decline.
- Premiers and prime ministers intentionally create cabinets to try to reflect the population.

Weaknesses

- Although Canada's legislative assemblies are more reflective of their population in terms of gender, occupation, and ethnicity than ever before, they are still a long way from being truly reflective of the Canadian demographic.
- Large swings against incumbent parties at election time are more likely than are internal actions by political parties to increase the number of women inside legislative assemblies.
- The appointed Senate contains a larger percentage of women, Aboriginals, artists, and other traditionally underrepresented groups than does the democratically elected House of Commons.

ROLES IN THE ASSEMBLY

3

Chapter 2 argued that in terms of inclusiveness Canadian legislatures are moving in the right direction and are now more reflective of Canadian society than ever. But beyond the question of legislators reflecting society, representation is also a matter of how well (or poorly) officials perform their elected functions. This aspect of representation is less concerned with who legislators are and more concerned with what they do. Once elected, members face multiple tasks and responsibilities. Members also have their own goals and ambitions, most of these focused on cabinet and the opportunity to fully participate in the policy process. But while cabinet dominates Westminster assemblies, it is only one part of the legislative process. Legislative chambers are the sum total of all their members, and those not in cabinet have their own duties. In order to perform them fully they must have both the ability (in terms of institutional rules) and the personal willingness to engage effectively in the scrutiny, legislative, and representational functions.

This chapter examines the more senior roles or positions of influence in Canadian legislatures. The fusion of executive and legislature builds a natural hierarchy within Westminster assemblies. Yet the governance of Parliament should be nonpartisan and the property of all members of Parliament. The problem faced by assemblies is difficult:

how can members govern themselves, compete for positions of influence, and still maintain some independence from party leaders? Unfortunately for Canadian legislatures, this often proves an impossible task.

The analysis begins with an examination of the legislature itself and how speakers are chosen. The chapter then examines the more government-centred roles in the chamber, including selection to cabinet and parliamentary secretaries (or assistants). Some roles facilitate activity within the chamber, and positions such as whip and House leader can be used to perform parliamentary functions. In these latter areas Canadian legislatures do a poorer job of promoting independence from party leadership. Most senior roles are tied up in party rather than parliamentary functions. As a result, parliaments in Canada tend to reinforce party strength and solidarity within caucuses. All too often, the important number in the governance of legislatures is not the number of members, but the number of recognized parties. This does little to enhance the participatory opportunities of legislators.

As this chapter demonstrates, the administrative functions and control of the legislative agenda rests with those who have greater interest in maintaining partisan emphasis, namely House leaders, whips, and party leaders. Even more junior positions, such as parliamentary secretary posts, foster strong loyalty to the government leaders. These positions are treated as testing grounds for future cabinet ministers, and the individuals who hold them are unlikely to step outside their party lines. Participation inside the assembly is too often less about individual abilities and more about the positions of political parties.

Of course, governments must be able to move ahead with their legislative and policy agendas. It only makes sense in a Westminster parliament that positions with the greatest amount of policy influence are part of the government and that people holding these spots favour strong party discipline. But when almost all positions above private member either formally or informally encourage intraparty cohesiveness, the ability of all members to participate fully in legislative and scrutiny functions can be compromised.

Participation by Members

Legislatures are hierarchical. Although all members of Parliament share the same rights and privileges, the power vested in individual members varies widely. This is particularly true in Westminster assemblies, where the executive sits in the legislative body (Loewenberg and Patterson 1979, 32). While all members share basic opportunities to participate, the position that a member holds in a legislature is often the single most important determinant of the extent of his or her possible participation. In Canadian legislatures, cabinet is the position that offers both the greatest possible participation and the opportunity for individuals to realize their personal political ambitions (Docherty 1997, 94-7).

Because all members in a parliamentary system do not have equitable authority, the ability to fully participate in the chamber is asymmetrical. Though this might seem obvious to both passive and keen observers of Parliament it does point to a crucial distinction in understanding the issue of participation in assemblies. Specifically, we can ask who governs the assembly. Is it all members or those in cabinet who have the greatest policy influence? Next we can distinguish among the ability to participate, the governing of the administration of the chamber, and the purposes (both direct and indirect) of positions of authority within the legislative arena.

At first blush, this seems like a lot of questions and layers to unpack. Indeed, legislatures are complex institutions. Power is a relatively fluid concept that is attached to both individuals and positions. Further complicating the mix is the fact that some positions of influence and authority are often at odds with each other. Table 3.1 outlines which formal positions in the chamber provide opportunities to participate in policy and legislative functions and which positions serve (either formally or informally) to reinforce party discipline in the chamber. The first thing to note about Table 3.1 is that it is rather bottom-heavy: the positions of greatest participation are also those that tend to buttress party solidarity. As subsequent sections of this chapter will demonstrate, these are the most sought-after positions in

Table 3.1

Participation and party discipline in Canadian legislatures

Opportunity to participate in policy/legislation	Degree to which position reinforces party dominance/discipline		
	Low	Medium	High
Low	Speaker Deputy speaker	Caucus chairs Shadow cabinet	
Medium	Committee chairs Government private members	Parliamentary secretaries Deputy whip	Opposition House leaders Whip
High		Opposition party leaders	Cabinet Government House leader Prime minister

Source: Adapted from Docherty 1997.

Canadian legislatures. Further, those who obtain a cabinet post, or serve as a House leader or whip, must demonstrate their loyalty to the party well in advance.

Whips and House leaders have less ability to participate in legislative and policy functions than cabinet ministers do but are nonetheless key parliamentary players. In both government and opposition, these positions involve working closely with party leaders, and are viewed as senior party leadership positions. As such they reinforce party dominance in the legislative setting.

Other posts that provide fewer occasions for participation policy making are important in terms of the accountability and scrutiny functions. Committee chairs perform valuable roles in facilitating discussion, allowing witnesses to present views to the government, and providing alternative policy options and positions to the government via their committees. Although the activities of committees are inclined to separate along party lines, a strong committee, given the proper circumstances, can transcend typical partisan concerns (Franks 1987, 165). An independent committee chair can facilitate nonpartisan discussion and cooperation on matters that might be off the government's radar screen. The problem is the limited ability of committees to enforce their reports or even work them onto the government's agenda.

Roles in the Assembly

Their efforts are often hamstrung by those in positions that reinforce party dominance.

Finally, the speaker of a legislature in Canada enjoys a unique position. The speaker both serves the legislature and administers the chamber, but he or she has little role in increasing participation. Speakers also have little policy influence, and given their nonpartisan role this is only fitting. While they do little to increase party supremacy in the chamber, their ability to dilute party dominance is also circumscribed. As a result there are many more positions heightening party solidarity than there are encouraging inter- or cross-party cooperation.

The Election of a Speaker

The speaker rules the House in the sense that he or she must control members and direct the activities of the House both inside the chamber and out. Legislatures are self-governed. They are not controlled by premiers or prime ministers. In Canada they are typically ruled by a Board of Internal Economy, an all-party committee that is chaired by the speaker. The Board of Internal Economy sets the budget for the assembly, sets direction on the resources that are provided for members, and sets the internal policies of the Commons. Running an assembly is a large and complex operation: during the parliamentary year 2001-2, the Canadian House of Commons budgeted for expenses over $300 million (House of Commons 2002b). Of course, all boards are dominated by the governing party, but the actions taken by the board are not related to government legislation. In serving as chair of the board, the speaker acts both as the master and as the servant of the chamber. He or she is directly responsible for the proper administration of the legislature, aided by the clerk of the chamber, who acts as both a procedural expert and a deputy, but assembly policies are decided by the all-party board.

Within the legislative chamber the speaker has more direct control. Although the standing orders and routine proceedings delineate the proceedings of the chamber, the speaker enjoys tremendous authority over the legislature. Maintaining order in an arena that is specifically geared toward confrontation is no easy task. A speaker who is too partisan cannot sustain the legitimacy of the office; a speaker who is too dictatorial will likewise not hold the required confidence of all members. A weak speaker will allow the opposition to obstruct the government's agenda to the point of gridlock.

The need for independence is a difficult line for speakers to walk. They must make fair and objective rulings and like a judge make decisions based on precedent and laws (in this case standing orders), favouring neither the government nor the opposition. Yet speakers were elected in their riding on a party ticket and hope to be re-elected on that same ticket. They are politicians who are allowed be partisan only at election time. In theory, speakers should be above the partisan call of their peers. There has always been some general discussion of the proposal that speakers should run for re-election to the post, and not on a party ballot. In order to accommodate this Canada would probably have to follow the British convention, whereby the major parties do not contest the seat where the speaker is running (Levy 1986, 11). A further and even larger complication in maintaining the nonpartisan nature of the office is the selection process of the speaker.

Until the fall of 1986 the speaker of the House of Commons was selected by the prime minister and ratified by all members of the chamber. Prime ministers generally tried to name a speaker who was acceptable to most members, yet the selection of a member to rule and serve all of the Commons was at best compromised by this partisan process. In some cases, while the individuals selected might have possessed some great talents, their expertise and sympathies did not always rest with the majority of backbenchers. The selection of Jeanne Sauvé in 1980 is a case in point (Levy 1986). Before Pierre Trudeau selected her as speaker, Sauvé had served her entire political career on the front benches, in cabinet. She had little understanding of the perspective of members who saw their chief roles as scrutiny and accountability.

In 1986, following committee recommendations for reform, the Mulroney government agreed to the direct election of a speaker by secret ballot. With the resignation of John Bosley in the fall the stage was set for this historic moment. The first election was long, arduous, and dramatic: it took eleven ballots and eleven hours to elect John Fraser (see Levy 1986). According to the standing orders, every member of the House of Commons who is not in cabinet or a party leader is a candidate for the position of speaker. Members who do not wish to be speaker must ask that their candidacies be withdrawn. After that, the process is very similar to party leadership contests. Ballots are held until someone reaches the magic 50 percent plus one, with the last-place candidate dropped from each ballot.

The fact that all candidates for the speaker's chair contest the same ballot is a consequential equalizer. At Westminster, recent experiments with election of the speaker have been far less equitable, and power still informally resides with the government. For example, the election of Speaker Martin in October 2000 proved more an embarrassment for the British Parliament than a step toward greater participation. The biggest problem was the rules governing the election. Instead of all candidates appearing on one ballot, each ballot placed the government's nominee against a single challenger (Strickland 2001). Unless a challenger could muster the support of a majority of members, the government's nominee would stand. The "mother of all Parliaments," Westminster, has now adopted a modified Canadian system for future elections.

The introduction of direct election has brought about a number of changes, not all of them positive. First, members of Parliament now actively and openly campaign to be speaker (Levy 1986). At the beginning of each new Parliament, those interested in the position lobby their colleagues and other party members in the hopes of gaining support. Yet despite the fears of former speaker John Bosley, this has not politicized the position. In fact, the opening up of the process has provided some transparency. All members of Parliament must seriously consider what type of Commons environment they wish to work within. Following the 2000 general election, some candidates for speaker, such as Roger Gallaway, put forth platforms for substantial parliamentary reform. Others, including the eventual speaker, Peter Milliken, argued that as a servant of the House, a speaker cannot lead the charge for parliamentary reform but rather should accommodate the desires of members to reform the legislature if that is the path most members wish to pursue (Taber 2001). The debate on the subject was not partisan, and members within parties disagreed over the direction and role of their next speaker. The fact that this debate was open and reported in national and regional newspapers can be seen as a positive development.

Second, the practice of alternating francophone and anglophone speakers is effectively over. Although this informal practice was breached only with the election of Speaker Fraser, it is difficult to maintain any custom when election dictates the outcome. Since Speaker Fraser's retirement, the tradition of electing speakers with at least a working knowledge of both official languages has been preserved. There are no guarantees that this will continue.

Third, electing the speaker after every general election makes it less likely that speakers will automatically serve subsequent terms. The historical goal of long-serving speakers – which was not achieved for much of Canada's history in any case (Levy 1986, 11) – can be challenged. Again, this is not necessarily negative. The re-election of Speakers Fraser, Parent, and Milliken can be interpreted as a vote of confidence by the majority of MPs, and not simply by the government. Although election turnover produces some new members who will have no real memory of an incumbent speaker, the re-election process does increase the level of the speaker's accountability.

Provincial assemblies followed the lead of the federal House, though some moved more quickly than others to elect their speakers. By 1989 Ontario had changed its standing orders to allow for direct and secret ballot election of speakers, and following the 1990 election, David Warner became the first directly elected speaker in that province. Saskatchewan moved two years later, and by 1999 all provinces had changed their standing orders to provide for direct elections. Nunavut and Northwest Territories have a secret election. Yukon does not.

These reforms to the selection of the speaker of the Canadian House of Commons, and subsequently in the provinces, have been nothing short of dramatic and positive for legislatures in Canada. The new procedure has both provided members of legislatures the opportunity to participate more fully in their self-governance, and strengthened the role of the speaker. Thus the reform has allowed all legislators, but particularly private members, to appreciate their independence from the executive.

One indication of the importance of the role of the speaker in a legislature is the stature of the individual serving in that role. In Ottawa, becoming speaker has historically been the pinnacle of a member's career. In the past quarter-century, only one speaker has continued as a member after serving in the chair. John Bosley continued to serve as an MP through the end of the term and indeed ran for re-election twice, successfully in 1988 and unsuccessfully in 1993. As a private member, he was active in committee and private member legislation.

Provincial representatives are more likely to see the speakership as a part of a political career (see Table 3.2). In Ontario, Chris Stockwell not only served in cabinet after leaving the speaker's chair but ran for the leadership of the provincial Progressive Conservative Party. This practice of former speakers eventually moving to cabinet is common provincially. Former speakers have yet to head a government, but not for lack of trying. John Reynolds was the speaker in the British Columbia legislature and served as interim leader of the Official Opposition in Ottawa in 2001. Former Nova Scotia speaker Ronald Russell moved from the objective chair in the middle of the legislature to sit at the right hand of Premier John Hamm as deputy premier following the 1999 general election. Len Sims of Newfoundland and Labrador served as speaker for nearly three years, beginning in 1979. He eventually became leader of the Progressive Conservative Party in that province. Like Jeanne Sauvé, some provincial speakers have also moved on to vice-regal posts. Legislatures that experience longer periods of one-party rule are more likely to have longer-serving speakers. Speaker Lloyd Snow in Newfoundland and Labrador and Speaker Ken Kowalski in Alberta have been serving for over seven and five years, respectively. Speaker Snow was originally appointed but was re-elected by secret ballot in 1999.

Table 3.2

Fate of former speakers in Canadian legislatures, 1978-2001

	House of Commons		Provinces and territories	
	Number	(%)	Number	(%)
Retired from office	1	16.6	16	21.1
Defeated in election	1	16.6	12	15.8
Received appointment	3	50.0	4	5.3
Moved to cabinet	0	0.0	19	25.0
Served as private member	1	16.6	25	32.9
Total	6		76	

Note: This table does not include speakers who were serving as of September 2002.
Source: Updated from Levy 1998.

Should we be concerned about the post-speaker career of a member? One possible apprehension is the question of independence. As indicated earlier, speakers make decisions based on precedent, not on their own partisan affiliations. If a speaker is thinking about a future appointment (either to cabinet or after retiring from Parliament), he or she might be inclined to make decisions that favour the government. Two points offer reassurance on this subject. First, the majority of speakers see their job as terminal or serve as private members after leaving the speaker's chair. Second, in the case of at least one speaker, the reverse was true. Most observers of Queen's Park during Premier Mike Harris's first term found Chris Stockwell to be an exceptionally independent speaker who was not afraid to criticize cabinet ministers and the premier for breaching parliamentary etiquette and privilege (Ontario 1997). In fact, he may have been offered a cabinet post specifically to remove him from the speaker's chair.

Nonetheless, there is some reason for concern. It is often difficult to decide what constitutes a "good" or "objective" speaker. Like a referee at a sporting event, a speaker's job evaluations often depend on whom any decision favours. Evident in Table 3.2 is the large number of speakers whose subsequent careers depend on some form of appointment. Fully one-half of former federal speakers received some form of external appointment. In the provinces and territories, one-quarter went on to serve in cabinet. For these members at least, the speakership might not be the pinnacle of a parliamentary career.

The Prime Minister and Selection to Cabinet

Although the speaker is the head of parliamentary government, there can be little doubt as to the head of elected government: the prime minister or premier. Cabinet is the apex of most legislators' political careers, and cabinet ministers are at the forefront of political life in Canada. The fusion of executive and legislature in parliamentary systems provides the lion's share of advantages to those on the front benches. Cabinet is the only place where legislators can engage in both the initiation and legislation of public policy.

In terms of both representation and participation, service in cabinet provides the greatest opportunity for legislators (Docherty 1997, ch. 4). Cabinet ministers represent not just their constituents or individuals who share certain demographic features, but also specific interests. The minister of agriculture is a representative for farmers and others employed in the agricultural industry. Moreover, ministers can spend money and direct programs to those areas they represent, an ability to participate in policy that is denied private members. Westminster parliaments do not allow private members to introduce legislation that would result in the direct expenditure of public monies. Only representatives of the Crown – namely cabinet ministers – enjoy this authority.

It is not much of a stretch to suggest that all members of Parliament seek a cabinet position. Most members hope for a cabinet career. Cabinet holds the greatest potential for rewarding both personal ambition and the desire to influence policy (Docherty 1997, 96). In the thirty-fourth Parliament (1988-93) over 80 percent of members surveyed stated that getting in cabinet was at least somewhat important to their career satisfaction. Among rookie MPs in the thirty-fifth Parliament (1993-7) the number was even higher at 84 percent (99). Interestingly the number dropped significantly in the thirty-seventh

Parliament (2000-4), in which just over 60 percent indicated that getting into cabinet was important to career success.

The reasons for this rather large drop are not altogether clear, though interview evidence suggests a combination of many factors. First, the timing of the questionnaire sent to members by the author is critical. The survey of members in the thirty-seventh Parliament was sent in 2001. Members of the Opposition had little short-term hope of forming the government. Second, Prime Minister Chrétien had a spotty record of shuffling his cabinet. His famous promise in 1993 that no one's job was safe seemed to diminish with time. As a result, many Liberal backbenchers, particularly those who favoured a different leader, did not have great prospects for advancement. Those with bleak prospects might view the brass ring as rather tarnished.

Nonetheless, almost two-thirds of responding MPs indicated in 2001 that cabinet was important. Such ambition is not surprising, but it does have its consequences. For one thing, members of cabinet are not involved in the scrutiny or accountability function of Parliament if they can avoid it. Given the adversarial nature of Westminster legislatures, members of the executive naturally seek to advance their legislation and policies with as little opposition as possible. If cabinet members can avoid the scrutiny of their own caucus and the opposition parties, they will. So parliamentary government creates its own unique paradox. The legislative body is supposed to act as a watchdog on government, yet the juiciest jobs are in the executive arm of the legislature. Thus members arrive in the capital to be watchdogs, but most of them would gladly give up this role for a seat at the cabinet table – where they hope to circumvent the scrutiny function. Given the plum that is cabinet, most ambitious politicians will presumably gear their behaviour inside the legislature to those activities that are most conducive to promotion.

Compounding this problem is the method by which cabinet ministers are selected. In all Canadian legislatures save the Northwest Territories and Nunavut, the premier or prime minister has complete freedom in creating the cabinet. In the two exceptions, all members vote on cabinet appointees (White 2005). Ideally, talent and expertise are the criteria for selecting members of the executive. Unfortunately, as with most things political, there is often a sizable gulf between the ideal and the real. Premiers, particularly in provinces with smaller legislatures, have a limited pool of individuals to choose from. Leaders can appoint cabinet members from outside the legislature, but there can be political costs to relying too heavily on this method. Prime ministers have a slightly larger pool. The House is more than twice as big as the largest provincial assembly, so the government caucus tends to be much bigger. Moreover, the prime minister can turn to the Senate for cabinet ministers, though this has occurred only rarely since 1980.

When selecting cabinet ministers from within the governing caucus prime ministers often have to place talent and expertise aside in favour of more immediate political considerations. Gender, ethnicity, and language are critical in Canadian politics (Smith 1997). In a nation as demographically, geographically, linguistically, and ideologically diverse as Canada, cabinets should be inclusive, given the problems outlined in Chapter 2. But there can be costs associated with the pursuit of diversity. Often a prime minister has to overlook someone with particular skills in order to make cabinet as representative as possible. A new member with a great deal of talent from Toronto, for example, might have a long wait for a cabinet seat. However, the only member of the governing party from a smaller province is almost guaranteed at least a minor portfolio. This practice might be good politics but it does not necessarily build a sense of professionalism or of rewarding hard work within the caucus. The same practice and associated pitfalls exist to a lesser degree at the provincial level.

While it may make political sense for prime ministers to look outside of caucus for a new cabinet member, it sends a troubling message to elected members that no one internal has the desired skills or political touches. Ambitious politicians infer that their leader is not interested in promoting from within. Equally damaging to caucus is the perception that even demographic characteristics are secondary to personal relations with the leader. The history of external appointments is mixed. Prime Minister Chrétien successfully went outside caucus in 1998 to bring in two cabinet ministers from Quebec, Pierre Pettigrew and Stéphane Dion, both of whom were subsequently appointed to Paul Martin's minority government cabinet in 2004. In perhaps the most infamous example since the Second World War, Prime Minister Brian Mulroney parachuted the ambassador to France, Lucien Bouchard, into the environment portfolio in 1986. Eventually Bouchard left the Conservative Party and headed two Quebec independence parties, the federal Bloc Québécois and the provincial Parti Québécois. The Conservatives are still living with the consequences.

Prime ministers may feel motivated to make cabinet representative of the Canadian public, but the public itself sees this as less important. Canadians were asked what factors a prime minister should use when selecting cabinet, while MPs were asked what factors they thought prime ministers actually used when selecting their executive. Table 3.3 illustrates the differences in their perceptions, which are noteworthy and substantial. Perhaps not surprisingly, members of Parliament think that prime ministers emphasize personal loyalty over expertise. Members of the thirty-seventh Parliament thought that national leaders ranked region higher than expertise. If this is indeed the case, it is a priority Canadians do not seem to favour. By a large margin, the public would like their cabinet ministers to be selected based on merit. There was also consensus that region should be an important criterion.

Table 3.3

How prime ministers choose (and should choose) cabinet ministers

	MPs in 35th Parliament (1993)	MPs in 37th Parliament (2001)	Canadian public (2000)	
			Ranking	% popularity of ranking
Expert in policy	2	3	1	35.1
Region represented	3	2	2	22.7
Seniority	5	4	3	15.0
Demographic background	4	5	4	14.9
Loyalty to leader	1	1		

Note: Percentages for public are popularity of that ranking; in each case it was a plurality. The public was asked to rank four choices, while MPs were provided a fifth alternative, loyalty to leader.
Sources: Author's surveys of MPs, 1993 and 2001; Canadian Election Study 2000.

Some public self-interest may be involved in this response, as no one wants their region unrepresented at the cabinet table. Neither demographic characteristics nor seniority were considered important criteria by Canadians (unfortunately, the survey did not include the question of loyalty to leader).

Note that Table 3.3 compares how MPs think prime ministers *actually choose* cabinet ministers to how Canadians think prime ministers *should choose* cabinet ministers. Members are obviously cynical about the practice of cabinet selection. If this cynicism is well founded (as suggested by the fact that these rankings held true across parties) then cabinet selection may have some negative impact on participation. When bypassing sitting members with talent, leaders are implicitly suggesting that there is no reward for becoming an expert in a policy field. The problem of course is that while there might not be a personal reward (i.e., promotion to cabinet) for this behaviour, there is a need. Scrutiny demands a certain level of knowledge of the policy fields of government. Policy experts do a much better job of the accountability function. Yet the message many members are receiving is that they are better off currying favour with their leader than being an effective policy entrepreneur. Another problem is the gulf that is created between public expectations and political reality. Canadians want experts in charge of government departments. The men and women serving as the political heads of these bureaucracies may well have skills, but that may not be the reason they are chosen.

On the other side, the practice of privileging factors other than expertise has one indirect benefit. If a prime minister is passing over talent when selecting his or her cabinet, then that talent remains on the backbenches, where the bulk of the accountability and scrutiny function takes place. Prime ministers may not reward the development of policy expertise, yet members with such skills can still make their presence felt. In fact, to keep the executive accountable, ideally there should be a healthy cohort of such individuals in both the opposition parties and the backbenches of government.

A prime minister's selections can eventually harm the leader. The move to leadership conventions in 1919 meant that party leaders could correctly argue that they answered to the rank and file of the party and not to the caucus (Courtney 1995). Before the development of leadership conventions, a party caucus selected the leader and always held the implicit threat of removal. The move to one person, one vote leadership contests has increased the ability of a leader to speak beyond his or her caucus. In many ways this decreases the authority of individual members of cabinet or caucus.

Nevertheless, a prime minister (or premier) cannot govern without the support of his or her caucus. While this is a rare situation in Canada, it does happen, as in the summer of 2002. The events that led to Jean Chrétien's eventual resignation announcement might seem to have begun with the departure of Minister of Finance Paul Martin in July 2002. There is reason to believe, though, that the problems began earlier. Having taken office in 1993 with the promise of frequent cabinet changes, Chrétien proceeded to have very few shuffles. The result was a feeling among many Liberal MPs, particularly those supporting others for the leadership, that they would never be in a Chrétien cabinet. Once backbenchers decided they would never get along, they had far less incentive to go along.

This was a positive development. During the lead-up to Chrétien's announced retirement it was clear that he had not distinguished between his own personal goals and the broader public interest (Radwanski 2002). It is a sign of a healthy parliamentary democracy that a majority of his caucus eventually caused him to understand that blurring of personal and public interest. The prime minister could not remove the problem simply by continually firing disloyal cabinet ministers. At the same time, the constant threat of resignations and the indefinite tenure of the prime minister detracted from a Parliament that was supposed to be involved in scrutiny and legislative functions. Caucus members were challenging their leader, but not for reasons prescribed by their parliamentary duties. The prime minister was not challenged over questions of ethics and unaccounted advertising in Quebec, but over the inability of some members to get promoted and the fighting among leadership challengers.

Finally, it is worth mentioning one disturbing feature of Canadian political careers, namely the so-called boomerang effect, which describes MPs who turn to provincial political careers. Studies of US politicians often demonstrate a linear career path from local to state to national politics. This path is usually the result of rational calculations of politicians about the right time to challenge for a specific office and the attractiveness of the office they seek (see for example Jacobson and Kernell 1983; Hibbing 1991). Only rarely do members of Congress move back to state office. This is at least partially due to the opportunities available in the US House of Representatives and Senate to become influential both politically and in terms of public policy. These opportunities have led Burdett Loomis (1988) to term some members of Congress "policy entrepreneurs," who can translate their interest and knowledge of a particular policy field into a position of power and authority on a committee.

Canada offers few opportunities for similar careers. The chance of gaining authority and public profile outside of cabinet is rare. As a result, some talented backbench and opposition MPs are tempted to step off the national stage onto the provincial one, where the opportunity for advancement is greater. For example, in 1998 NDP MP Chris Axworthy left Ottawa for a more realistic chance of becoming a cabinet minister in an NDP Saskatchewan government. His gamble paid off. Bob Rae of Ontario and Pat Binns and Catherine Callbeck of Prince Edward Island left critic and other noncabinet roles in the House to lead their provincial parties, and then became premiers. Lucien Bouchard, Russell MacLellan, and Jean Charest left front-bench positions in Ottawa to lead provincial parties and form governments.

Is this trend worrisome? The departure of a few members for the provinces is not dramatic, nor does it signal the decline of the federal Parliament. However, the success rate of MPs who leave Ottawa to serve provincially is interesting. Among other things it suggests that many members who do not serve in cabinet have trouble creating enjoyable careers. Further, it reinforces the perception that there is little desirable in a parliamentary career. Parliament seems to do a better job of losing talent than it does retaining it.

Parliamentary Secretaries and the Problem of Participation

If cabinet is the brass ring of elected life, other positions are far down the list in terms of attractiveness. Parliamentary secretary is one such posting. Parliamentary secretaries assist ministers in policy formation, help steer legislation through the chamber, and occasionally answer questions in the House (Docherty 1998). The position, created temporarily during the two world wars but continued during the postwar governments of Mackenzie King and beyond, was designed to allow members of Parliament to assist cabinet ministers in their duties (Ward 1987, 169). Beyond assisting cabinet, parliamentary secretaries had an opportunity to learn about a particular ministry and demonstrate their skills to the prime minister. As the position evolved, it began to be seen as a training ground for potential cabinet ministers. Hopefully, when cabinet openings occurred, competent parliamentary secretaries would be the first in line for promotion.

As Peter Dobell (2001, 12) points out, parliamentary secretaries continued in this role without much interruption until the Trudeau era. Secretaries served for long periods, but did so knowing they would eventually be promoted to the front benches. Trudeau's introduction of set two-year terms of office for parliamentary secretaries changed all of this. The practice of "permanent rotation" was meant to provide more MPs with occasions to gain semi-administrative experience and demonstrate their capabilities. Unfortunately the result was far less positive than anticipated. It has not helped recent parliaments that Jean Chrétien adopted the Trudeau practice. Between their tenures, Brian Mulroney did not believe in automatic rotation, and reappointed parliamentary secretaries he thought were effective in their roles (ibid., 12).

Being appointed parliamentary secretary is seen as a consolation prize instead of a promotion (Hutchison 2000). Many members do not enter the office thinking they have been given an opportunity to prove their worth, but rather concluding that they have been passed over

(Glenn 1997). And if members who are appointed to a secretaryship believe that it is tantamount to winning a distant second prize, the impact on those who are passed over for this position (perhaps more than once) is even more devastating. It signals a career that is going nowhere fast.

Among the more critical problems with rotation is that departments have little incentive to bring parliamentary secretaries inside the loop. As MP Reg Alcock explains, why would a department spend time and energy developing policy skills in a parliamentary secretary who will be gone in two years (in Dobell 2001, 9)? The short tenure of parliamentary secretaries is not unique to the Chrétien government. In fact, parliamentary secretaries under the Chrétien and Trudeau administrations served on average as long as parliamentary secretaries under King and Pearson, one and a half years (Hutchison 2000, 23), though shorter parliaments characterized the Pearson administration.

But the constant rotation causes problems of morale. Effective parliamentary secretaries see themselves as legitimate cabinet ministers in waiting. In the opinion of Clifford Lincoln, a cabinet minister in the National Assembly of Quebec prior to turning to federal politics, the two-year nonrenewable hitch sends all the wrong signals: "When I received the Prime Minister's letter advising me in such lofty and sincere language that I had served my country with intelligence, nobility, dedication and utmost efficiency ... I could not help but wonder why, had I been so proficient, I was being fired at the same time" (in Dobell 2001). Members' notion that they are informed of their demotion essentially by form letter hardly builds esprit de corps (Hutchison 2000, 23).

Lincoln's rather blunt comment sums up the contradiction inherent in the policy of rotating parliamentary secretaries. Good members are going to be angry with the results. In addition, the position becomes less valued as members realize it is no step to future promotion. MPs realize that they are being made a parliamentary secretary not because the prime minister is looking for talent but simply because it is time for a regular rotation. Further, after good members lose positions as parliamentary secretaries, where are they going? The answer creates its own problems. Some become committee chairs, but this only disrupts the work and continuity of committees.

Even without continual rotation, the position of parliamentary secretary can compromise the scrutiny function of the Commons. A parliamentary secretaryship is a quasi-executive position. Parliamentary secretaries are below the rung of ministers of state, but certainly higher than committee chairs, regional caucus chairs, or other such positions. Parliamentary secretaries do not have the power of cabinet to introduce money bills, but they are considered part of the government in many important respects. They work as right-hand support people for ministers during passage of legislation. According to David Hutchison (2000, 23), the ties to the minister's office are so close that when it comes to second or third reading of a bill, many parliamentary secretaries receive "a prepared speech by electronic mail from the Minister's department." Parliamentary secretaries' participation in legislative proceedings is thus tantamount to that of an arm of the executive, not the legislature.

Therefore, when parliamentary secretaries are included with the cabinet, we have vastly increased the number of members who approach scrutiny from the opposite side of the fence, namely with the aim of avoiding it. In 2002 there were twenty-eight full ministers (including the prime minister), ten secretaries of state, and twenty-seven parliamentary secretaries. This means that of the Liberal caucus of 170, fully 65 were in positions that spent more effort avoiding scrutiny than engaging in it.

The role and function of the parliamentary secretary is therefore slightly puzzling. In theory the position should serve as a training ground for future cabinet ministers. In reality the track record is far from good. Of individuals who served as parliamentary secretaries in the thirty-fifth Parliament, only three had ended up in cabinet by the thirty-seventh Parliament, two of those as secretaries of state. Parliamentary secretaries are provided some opportunity to become policy experts, but their short tenure in that office discourages officials from dedicating much energy to educating them. Members return to caucus with less salary, less power, and a sense that they are back where they started. While parliamentary secretaries serve important functions, from the standpoint of the Audit value of participation, it should be remembered that they serve executive and not legislative responsibilities.

Whips and House Leaders

The positions of party whip and House leader are directly involved in fostering strong party solidarity. The House leader typically sits on the Board of Internal Economy as his or her party's representative, but the primary function of a House leader is to facilitate the passage of legislation and the other business of the House. House leaders of all parties meet to set the agenda for each week. Though the government House leader has the ultimate authority over the legislative agenda, cooperation among parties is usual to ensure that the appropriate critics, parliamentary secretaries, and cabinet ministers are available to discuss pending legislation. On questions of privilege and points of order, House leaders are unabashed advocates for the rights of their members. On questions of the legislative agenda they act more as representatives of their party. A strong working relationship among opposition House leaders can be an effective tool for stalling or stealing the government's agenda. In the recent multiparty parliaments in Ottawa, such cooperation has been a prerequisite of effective accountability. When opposition parties are working at cross-purposes, the government can more easily deflect criticism from one party by playing it against another. House leaders prefer strong party discipline, but for them it is a means to an end, namely a legislative timetable and agenda that works in their parties' best interests.

Party whips answer more directly to the party leader. Their function is straightforward: whips ensure that their appropriate caucus colleagues are in committee, in the chamber during debate, and available for votes. The title "whip" appropriately suggests that their role is to whip members into line — or more accurately to solidify caucus solidarity on votes. The term is thought to originate in Great Britain and derive from the "whippers-in" at fox hunts, charged with keeping the numerous hounds in order (Silk and Walters 1995, 47).

On the government side of the House, whips are not typically members of cabinet, but work closely with the House leader, as part of their role involves coordinating members' time. The fundamental requirement of the government is that it must know it enjoys the confidence of the chamber at all times. In cases of majority governments, this means the government must have a numeric advantage in the chamber. This is rarely an issue during the daily question period when attendance is quite high. However, during debate on bills, committee of the whole, and other proceedings, attendance in the chamber slips dramatically. The role of the whip is to make sure his or her party (particularly the party in power) is not caught off-guard. Whips also safeguard against poor party attendance in committees. If a party is not represented in a committee, amendments to bills can be passed, important witnesses can appear, and agendas can change all without the involvement of a party. The whip protects against such occurrences.

Beyond their coordination function, whips provide communication between party leadership and members of caucus. Whips must know where caucus members stand on issues before the chamber or committee, in order to have a sense of where problems of solidarity might arise. Whips are therefore in constant communication with members and their staffs (Franks 1987, 106). Whips try to anticipate potential problems and resolve them before they become public. This may mean manipulating a member's schedule to send him or her out of town for a vote on which the MP does not share the party's view.

In Canada the role of the whip is somewhat easier than it is in Great Britain. The Parliament at Westminster employs what is known as a three-line whip system. On a one-line whip, caucus members are expected either to vote along party lines or, if they choose to dissent, to inform the whip's office. On a two-line whip, a member should be "twinned" with a dissenting member from another party (an arrangement where the two absences effectively cancel each other out). When a three-line whip is in effect, members are simply "expected to turn up and vote on the matter under discussion" (Silk and Walters 1995, 48). In Canada there are no distinctions among levels of the whip. With few exceptions, all matters are considered votes of confidence in the government, making them the equivalent of a three-line whip. While whips in Canada must communicate with the caucus members, the nuances of what any particular piece of legislation means to the success of government are not part of the discussion. One result is that Canadian whips spend more time communicating down than they do up. Thus this important position helps to secure strength behind the party leader.

Conclusion

In theory, Parliament and provincial legislatures are self-governing bodies. All are administered by some version of an all-party Board of Internal Economy that establishes the budget of the legislature and the staffing and resources available for members. All members share equal rights and privileges. However, as with most things there is a substantial gap between theory and practice.

First, the Board of Internal Economy and its decisions favour parliamentary parties over members of Parliament. While all members are provided basic staff and global allowances, additional resources are given to parties that have a minimum caucus of twelve (Blaikie 1994). The number twelve, a creature of the Board of Internal Economy, encourages the fostering of party ties and discourages minor parties in the Commons. The experience of the Democratic Reform Caucus, a temporary breakaway group of Alliance MPs in 2001-2, is telling. Without twelve members, they were unable to sustain themselves and gain access to full parliamentary resources, because they simply were not considered a party. This rule excludes certain members from full participation. During the thirty-fifth Parliament, the two-member caucus of the formerly governing Conservatives did not meet the criteria for full participation (Docherty 1998). In subsequent elections, the NDP and Conservatives have strived to achieve the magic, but purely arbitrary, number twelve.

Of course those who govern legislative chambers in Canada do not necessarily govern all members. Speakers both run and are servants of the assembly. But real political power rests elsewhere. While the focus of the legislature should be centred on those functions that demand accountability from the government, the reality is often far different. Most members seek positions in cabinet, whose members hope to avoid accountability (at least in its most raw form) more than they embrace it. The Canadian Parliament does not encourage government private members to scrutinize the cabinet openly through participation in formal roles. Instead, it rewards individuals who are loyal to their leader in two significant ways.

First, promotion is determined by party leaders. As a result, with few exceptions – and usually these involve individuals with a significant personal support base in the extraparliamentary party – positions of influence are granted to those who support the prime minister's leadership. Second, these promotions entail financial incentives in the form of additional salaries that also affect pensions. There is no monetary advantage in being an effective committee chair. As a result, even effective chairs may be tempted to leave their post to accept a limited term as a parliamentary secretary. This is unfortunate because good committee chairs can make a substantial contribution to the democratic discourse within a legislature. The history of committees is admittedly spotty, but they can produce thoughtful contributions to public policy and debate (this is discussed further in Chapter 7). As long as other positions of authority remain higher on the list of opportunities to influence policy – and as long as these positions remain tied to party and leader solidarity – the chance that members will prefer committee work over parliamentary secretary, whip, and House leader jobs, let alone cabinet, remains a long shot.

If there are institutional disincentives for full participation inside Canadian assemblies, how do members fare away from their legislature? The next chapter looks at the representation that takes place primarily outside the assembly: how members represent their constituents, and what resources are available to members for this function.

CHAPTER 3

Strengths

♦ The secret ballot election of speaker in most Canadian assemblies is a relatively recent, and positive, development. In the House of Commons, the speakership is the pinnacle of a political career. This is less likely to be the case provincially.

♦ Good working relationships between House leaders ensures that the government can proceed with its legislative agenda while the opposition can scrutinize the government's plans.

Weaknesses

♦ The fusion of executive and legislature builds a natural hierarchy within Westminster assemblies. The most sought-after positions on both sides of the chamber tend to reinforce party discipline instead of promoting scrutiny and active participation.

♦ Most elected officials desire a cabinet career and see loyalty to their leader as the key criterion to being appointed to cabinet.

♦ With few exceptions, legislatures in Canada are organized around political parties and provide many resources for legislative activity to parties instead of to individual MPs.

4 CONSTITUENCY WORK

Constituency work is often overlooked by academics and criticized by those less favourable to politicians. Members are portrayed as ward heelers or pork-barrel politicians bringing home the bacon. The clichés are endless. But the job of local representation is a critical feature of a Westminster parliamentary system, particularly one based on single-member districts. Representing constituents – either individuals or groups in the riding – is one of the largest jobs of Canadian legislators.

The term "good constituency man" is historical not simply because of the gendered language. It reflects a rose-coloured view of a past when members were interested first in helping constituents, second in voicing constituents' views in Ottawa (or the provincial capital), third in debating national (or provincial) issues, and fourth and finally, hoping this might help them get re-elected. Whether or not that was true in the past, there is no evidence that many members do not take this approach today. In fact, both provincially and federally, Canadian parliamentarians are true constituency people. Members spend an extraordinary amount of time and effort on local work. Members may be shut out of meaningful policy participation in their legislatures – but they have plenty of scope to act at home. The majority of members make the most of this opportunity. Doubtless thoughts of re-election are never far from the minds of MPs and MLAs, and many members do relate local work to their upcoming re-election bids. But they engage in local activities knowing that this will not lock up electoral security. Instead they participate in local work for one of the noblest reasons of all, because it needs to be done.

When members act in the capital they wear a number of hats, but in the constituency their role is clear. Almost universally, members are advocates on behalf of their constituents, plain and simple (Docherty 1997, 174-7). When it comes to individual casework, or helping a local group deal with government bureaucracy, legislators are unapologetic voices on behalf of their people. In this role a member is the quintessential small businessperson, and the constituent who goes to a constituency office might as well be entering the proprietor's store: no matter what the view, the customer is always right.

For some members this approach is a learned response. For example, many rookie members of the Reform Party first arrived in Ottawa in 1993 with a rather skeptical view of those seeking benefits from the government. However, once faced with constituents who had problems obtaining legitimate services, Reform/Alliance members were as willing as any MP to help them. Indeed, many quickly turned their anger toward Ottawa and the civil service for not being more responsive to citizens.

Members maintain contact with their constituencies (and constituents) in a variety of manners. Federally, and in most provinces and territories, members have a constituency office. These are staffed with either full-time employees or volunteers, and serve as a community help office within the riding. Legislators have budgets for mailing, and are often provided with funds to send "householders" – quarterly or biannual newsletters – that inform voters what their representative is doing on their behalf, both at home and in the capital. Members from rural or smaller communities often write columns in local papers. Members hold town hall meetings and regular office hours while in the constituency. In addition, federal and provincial members are expected to attend local events that run the gamut from discussions of national matters (say, the appropriateness of gay marriages or sending Canadian troops to Iraq) to attending an eighty-fifth birthday in a nursing home with greetings from the prime minister or premier.

In addition to this, members (and their constituency offices) are expected to act as local ombudspersons. In urban downtown ridings, federal members claim that their offices are unofficial immigration bureaus, and some argue with conviction that they can correlate cuts in the federal immigration department to large increases in the number of immigration cases they handle. Provincial and territorial members field questions on education, health care, social assistance, and worker compensation, all policy areas controlled by their level of government. Members also assist voters in a myriad of other ways, such as helping seniors with taxes, assisting local organizations to obtain funding for projects, and developing economic infrastructures. Members of legislatures are the day-to-day filter or link between many citizens and the state. This chapter examines the environment surrounding constituency work in Canada, including the challenges faced by members and the resources provided by assemblies to assist members in this function.

Challenges of Size

One of the first problems potentially faced by members of a legislature is how many citizens live in their district. The more voters, the more demands there will be on a member. In addition, although elected officials represent people and not rocks and trees, the physical size of a riding can produce its own inefficiencies. Work in a large rural (or northern) riding is a much different experience from servicing a more heavily populated and compact urban or suburban riding. In the country, there may be fewer constituents to seek a member's services, but getting to the riding office – or visiting the constituent's house – can be almost as arduous as dealing with the actual problem. In the city, the number of events that must be attended, and the number of calls and visits to the riding, might more than make up for the ease of travel.

In terms of actual population per district, Canada is similar to other nations. The best comparison is probably Australia, which has a comparable total population and physical size. While the average number of constituents per district is higher in Australia (132,048 compared to 107,220), however, our range is much greater. Canada's most populous electoral district has over seven times the population of our smallest. In both the United States and Australia, the largest district is not quite twice the size of the smallest. The range of populations in Canadian districts is due in part to protections we give to smaller provinces to ensure they do not lose seats at redistribution. Those charged with drawing boundaries are also allowed a wider variation of population per riding. Electoral districting is discussed in detail in John Courtney's volume (2004) of this audit.

In each of these three countries, federal constituencies do not cross provincial or state lines. Of course each subnational unit must also have at least one seat. In Canada the federal riding with the smallest population is therefore Nunavut. In the United States this has led to extremes of a different sort. Very small states – such as Wyoming, with a population of less than 500,000 – have one member of Congress. So do larger states that are not quite entitled to two representatives – such as Montana, with a population of over 900,000. The responsibilities of each member are the same although the number of their constituents varies widely. There are also physical considerations. Roughly speaking there is an inverse relationship between the physical size of a riding and its population. With the exception of Prince Edward Island, most of the less populous ridings are incredibly large.

Canadian constitutional and statutory protections for smaller provinces have meant that each province has its own electoral quotient (or average population per district). In terms of number of constituents, MPs in Ontario, Alberta, and British Columbia are the busiest. These are the only provinces whose electoral quotients approximate the national quotient (obtained by dividing the population by the number of seats in the House of Commons; see Table 4.1). In just about every other case (save Quebec), the subnational quotient is substantially lower than the national quotient.

At first blush one might be tempted to draw a strong relationship between the number of constituents and constituency workload. More

Table 4.1

Population of federal and provincial constituencies, 2001

Province	Population	House of Commons seats	Federal electoral quotient	Seats in provincial/ territorial assembly	Average number of citizens per provincial district
Newfoundland and Labrador	512,930	7	73,276	48	10,686
Prince Edward Island	135,294	4	33,824	27	5,010
Nova Scotia	908,007	11	82,546	52	17,462
New Brunswick	729,498	10	72,950	55	13,264
Quebec	7,237,479	75	96,500	125	57,900
Ontario	11,410,046	106	107,642	103	110,777
Manitoba	1,119,583	14	79,970	57	19,462
Saskatchewan	978,933	14	69,924	58	16,878
Alberta	2,974,807	28	106,243	83	35,841
British Columbia	3,907,738	36	108,548	79	49,465
Northwest Territories	37,360	1	37,360	19	1,966
Nunavut	26,745	1	26,745	19	1,408
Yukon	28,674	1	28,674	18	1,593
Total (national quotient)	30,007,094	308	107,220		

Note: To maintain consistency, population figures from Elections Canada based on the 2001 census have been used throughout the table.
Source: Elections Canada 2002.

voters should equal more phone calls. While this is generally the case, the problem behind each phone call is not equally easy to solve. The type of concern a voter brings to a constituency office in rural Newfoundland or northern Manitoba will be very different and might require more effort than the concern of an Ontarian living in the 905 belt surrounding Toronto. Further, just about every MP believes that his or her riding office is among the busiest in the country (Docherty 1997).

Within Canada, the number of seats in provincial assemblies varies, though less widely than their populations do. Provincial assemblies range from an average of just over 5,000 residents per district in PEI to an average of over 110,000 residents in Ontario ridings (see Table 4.1). It is not surprising that the smallest and largest provinces have the least and most populous districts, respectively. Inversions in seat totals occur in more than one instance (Alberta, for example, has a smaller population but more seats than British Columbia; likewise for Saskatchewan and Manitoba, and New Brunswick and Nova Scotia). But the relationship between population of province and its districts is relatively clear. Larger jurisdictions have larger assemblies, but the larger assemblies do not equalize the number of residents per legislator. A rather large variation among jurisdictions still exists.

Resources for Constituency Work

So how do members meet the needs of their voters at the local level? For the most part, the ability of members to respond to constituency concerns is a product of the resources legislatures provide. And most legislatures have made strong efforts to provide members with the services necessary to properly perform constituency services. Canadian constituency service has become highly professionalized. The days of the member of Parliament, known by one and all in the riding – and always willing to help at any time of day or night (much like the romanticized country vet) – may belong more in our mythology than in history books. Nonetheless, modern federal members have made up for this with increased resources directed specifically at serving constituents. The professionalization of politics in Canada and the advent of the professional politician have brought many changes, not just in Canada's national chamber but in every jurisdiction in Canada.

The development of a more professional constituency office was evolutionary and began some time after what may be considered the beginning of the modern parliamentary era in the 1950s (Power 1957). What constitutes the modern Parliament in Canada is not altogether clear, and debated by some with perhaps too much time on their hands. It is probably more appropriate to understand that no single point in time ushered in a "modern era" of Parliament in Canada. During the late 1950s and early 1960s more services were provided to members in the Commons, the chamber met more often, and many members began to treat their elected position as a full-time job, not just a part-time calling. At the same time, many MPs still maintained ties to businesses or law firms in their constituencies and depended on an outside

Table 4.2

Constituency services in Canadian legislatures

Province	Allowance for constituency office?	Annual allowance for staff/office	Freedom to allocate staff?
House of Commons	Yes	Global staff and supplies budget for Ottawa and constituency $214,000-272,000	Yes
Senate	No	$137,000	n/a
Newfoundland and Labrador	No constituency office provided	One political assistant provided for each member	Yes
Prince Edward Island	Regional centres available for constituency work	MLAs provided with caucus staff and office	No
Nova Scotia	Yes	$48,600	Yes
New Brunswick	Yes	$25,000	Yes
Quebec	Yes	$104,000-122,000	Yes
Ontario	Yes	$153,350	Yes
Manitoba	Yes	$41,925	Yes
Saskatchewan	Yes	$38,868	Yes
Alberta	Yes	$69,035 (average based on funding formula)	Yes
British Columbia	Yes	2.5 full-time staff	Yes

Sources: Legislative websites; author's survey of provincial and territorial legislative clerks, 2002.

source of income to supplement their parliamentary pay. Well into the 1960s members did not have official constituency offices with paid staff. Their spouses typically acted as constituency secretaries. Meetings with constituents would often take place in the MP's home, and problems were not resolved until after the next return trip from Ottawa.

Today, an MP has at least one office in the riding, an allowance that allows for up to four staff to be divided between the capital and the constituency, and complete computer, e-mail, fax, and other services between Ottawa and home. Indeed, members are allotted resources in a more uniform manner than they are allotted constituents. The same types of services are provided to members of most provincial legislatures as well (see Table 4.2). Despite the fact that senators are appointed to represent regions, no such local facilities are provided to members of Canada's upper house.

By contrast, US members of the House of Representatives have a much larger budget that allows for up to eighteen permanent staff. Of course most US federal districts have approximately six and a half times the population of Canadian federal constituencies. US senators have a more varied set of resources. Senators from larger states (over 28 million people) each have a staff allowance of $2.3 million. Even senators from small states receive a $1 million staff allowance (Congressional Research Service Report 1999). But Canadian MPs fare better than their UK counterparts. It was only with the completion of a second parliamentary building in 2000 that every member of Parliament had an office at Westminster (Rush 2001, 126). Most British MPs have one full-time assistant in Westminster and up to one full-time equivalent in the constituency. Some British members supplement their constituency staff with volunteers (often party workers) or staff paid by outside sources such as the local party association or the members themselves.

Provincially, resources provided to Canadian legislators vary widely. Members in every province save Newfoundland and Labrador and Prince Edward Island are provided with enough funds to have a constituency office with at least one full-time staff. In Newfoundland, members are allotted one political assistant each, to deploy as they see fit. Taking advantage of its small geography and less populous ridings, Prince Edward Island employs regional service centres shared by more than one member of the assembly. Such an arrangement is not viable in other jurisdictions, where distance makes travelling across many constituencies impractical for individuals seeking assistance. The larger provincial assemblies in Ontario, Quebec, and British Columbia provide a large allowance that can be used as individual members determine. While most federal members split their staffs evenly between their Ottawa and riding offices, this pattern is less evident in the provinces, in large part due to the smaller staffing allowances provided. In some provinces the amount of funding for constituency staff is rather limited, and members of the New Brunswick assembly, for example, are quick to point out that they do not receive nearly enough to handle the demands of the job.

Given that provincial governments all have responsibility for the same policy areas (notably health, education, and social services), the type of constituency work should be relatively constant across jurisdictions. The problem-solving component of constituency work will primarily be a function of constituency size. In other words, a constituency that has 75,000 residents should be approximately three times as busy as one that has 25,000 citizens, no matter what provinces the ridings are in. This is an admittedly broad assumption. As discussed above, different parts of the country have their own unique challenges in terms of local representation. Nonetheless, we understand that within subnational constituencies the type of individual help provided by legislators is relatively constant.

One reason often cited for constituency work is re-election. In studies of the US Congress beginning with Mayhew (1974), political scientists have often argued that members' work both in the capital and constituency is geared toward this goal. While legislators are attracted to office for multiple reasons (Searing 1994; Fenno 1978; Docherty 2002c), re-election is a necessary prerequisite to any legislator's goals. Therefore members will avoid activity that might hinder their prospects for re-election, while engaging in activities that will help solidify their support at home. Different jurisdictions offer different rewards for local effort. In the United States, local work is seen to build a strong personal vote (Cain, Ferejohn, and Fiorina 1987). British members are less rewarded for local work, but safe constituencies still require personal attention (Searing 1994; Cain, Ferejohn, and Fiorina 1987). Further, while British MPs may have been slower than North American legislators to realize the value of constituency work, they have more than made up for this ignorance. Constituency service is increasingly becoming a focus of British legislators (Norton and Wood 1993; Rush 2001).

In Canada the electoral equation is much different. Neither provincially nor federally has the incumbency effect been strong (Irvine 1982; Docherty and White 1999). The conventional wisdom of Canadian constituency service is simple: while good constituency service is no guarantee of re-election, bad constituency service almost assures defeat. Nonetheless, many members believe that their strong local reputations help them at election time (Docherty 1997, 176-80). In close races, constituency service can make an important and vital difference. So members of legislatures in Canada must take their local service seriously. In addition, much of this work is demand driven: constituents see members as the one office in government they can turn to and expect a speedy, and concerned, response. Finally, most members express a great deal of enjoyment in this aspect of their work (Docherty 1997, 176-86). For most members, the largest concern is not the demand but the supply. That is, do members have the resources necessary to meet their constituents' needs?

Bridging the Distance to the Capital

For legislators, one of the largest challenges is simply getting back and forth between home and office. In some jurisdictions, Prince Edward Island for example, the problem of distance is relatively minor. With twenty-six constituencies covering 5,660 square kilometres, and a capital approximately in the middle of the province, MLAs have little difficulty travelling to and from Charlottetown and around their districts. The problem is somewhat greater for the federal member for Nunavut. Not only is the riding nearly 2 million square kilometres in area (approximately one-fifth the size of the entire country) but most communities do not have road access, and time needed to travel the riding is extraordinary. Plane travel is a way of life in providing constituency services. Getting to Ottawa is also difficult. The present member for Nunavut, Nancy Karetak-Lindell, has said that it is easier and quicker to fly from Ottawa to Europe than from Ottawa to her home in Arviat. When she travels to Ottawa on Saturdays, the route takes her through Winnipeg and Toronto. When she travels on Mondays, Wednesdays, or Fridays, she arrives in Ottawa via Rankin Inlet and Iqaluit (Member itinerary, August 2002).

Most jurisdictions provide members with both the means and the time to travel back and forth from their riding to the capital. Members of Parliament and MLAs have allowances for travel between the capital and home that vary according to the expense involved. Allowances equalize the playing field because members are not out of pocket for living and travel expenses. In Ottawa, the House of Commons began to build "constituency weeks" into its calendar in 1991 (Robertson 1991, 6). Regular breaks in the sitting schedule allow members to spend more uninterrupted time in their constituencies. Ideally, this means that members might spend some weekends in the capital, knowing that one week in four will be spent in the riding. Even so, most MPs return to their riding every weekend (Docherty 1997). The result is better responsiveness at home, but poorer attendance to legislative duties on Fridays. Soon after becoming leader of the Canadian Alliance in 2000, Stockwell Day mused that Friday sittings should be dispensed with because MPs take Thursday evening flights home. It was quickly realized that most members would simply leave Wednesday to have an additional full day for constituency activities. The idea was soon abandoned, even by Day.

The development of information technology has affected members of provincial and federal governments just as it has every other field. E-mail is another method available for the interaction of constituents and members. The websites of all Canadian legislatures provide direct e-mail access to their members, although the success of electronic contact in Canada is limited at best. Members of Parliament have been very slow to make use of web-based technology and even e-mail to reach voters within and external to their districts. In April 2003 two-thirds of MPs had functional websites. Why doesn't each MP have one? The reason appears to be a combination of lack of enthusiasm on the part of some members, and the problem faced in accounting for the political nature of websites. Interestingly, in 2002 the Alliance, which had long called for a more populist approach, had the highest percentage of websites among caucuses in Ottawa. Over 85 percent of Alliance MPs had sites, compared to 55 percent of Liberals, half of New Democrats, a third of the Bloc Québécois caucus, and only a quarter of the Conservative caucus (Crossing Boundaries National Council 2002; see also Jansen and Thomas 2003).

Compounding the problem is a lack of support for member websites by the House of Commons. In Great Britain and Australia, the parliamentary website contains direct links to the sites of individual members. This is not the case in Canada. Consequently members do not have uniform web addresses differentiated only by their names. It also makes it much more difficult for constituents, and others interested in contacting a member, to find the appropriate website.

The rationale for not having direct links to members' websites may be the potential for them to be too partisan, which would violate the nonpartisan restrictions that accompany the funding of constituency services for members. However, the House of Commons could provide funding for members' constituency-based sites just as it currently funds the "householders" that members regularly send to all homes in their ridings. The constituency-based sites, like the householders, would focus on questions of representation and deal with matters in the riding and in the Commons on a nonpartisan basis. Members could have two websites: a partisan one separate from the Commons, and one that serves as a virtual constituency office, providing interactive services and information. It is hard to imagine a negative consequence of increasing local services in this fashion – particularly in large, rural, or northern ridings where physically visiting a constituency office can be at best troublesome and at worst a full day's trip.

Of all the legislatures in Canada, the Senate has among the most liberal rules regarding members' personal websites. As Table 4.3 shows, it is the only jurisdiction in Canada in which the chamber's website provides direct links to its members' private sites. The Senate site includes a notice that the senators' own sites are "not part of the Parliamentary Internet Site." This disclaimer allows the Senate to provide the links without fear of funding partisan activities outside the chamber. Not only the House of Commons but all assemblies should consider this. On the downside, only fourteen senators have their own websites, so the access thus provided is limited.

While most legislatures in Canada provide members' pictures and biographies on the web, the quality of biographies and information varies. The House of Commons, for example, provides a picture, brief

Table 4.3

Assembly website links to members

	Direct links to members' e-mail	Biographies/ pictures of all members	Direct links to members' websites	Constituency address and capital address of all members provided
House of Commons	Yes	Yes	No	Both
Senate	Yes	Yes	Yes	Parliament only
Newfoundland and Labrador	Yes	Yes	No	Both
Prince Edward Island	Yes	No	No	Phone numbers only
Nova Scotia	Yes	Yes	No	Both
New Brunswick	Yes	Yes	No	Capital only
Quebec	Yes	Yes	Yes	Both
Ontario	Yes	Yes	Only through party sites	Both
Manitoba	Yes	Yes	No	Capital only
Saskatchewan	Yes	No	No, but links through caucus home pages	Both
Alberta	Yes	Yes	No	Both
British Columbia	Yes	Yes	Yes	Both
NWT	Yes	Yes	No	Both
Nunavut	Yes	Pictures but no biographies	No	Both
Yukon	Yes	Yes	No	Capital only

Sources: Legislative websites 2004.

biography, capital and constituency addresses, and a direct e-mail link to the member. There are direct links to the websites of each of the parties with seats in the assembly. More detailed information on members can be found on these sites, but it is party oriented and not necessarily geared toward local representation. Other sites, such as the Saskatchewan Legislative Assembly, provide no pictures and little information on members. Legislative websites in British Columbia and Nunavut provide not just pictures and addresses, but biographies of members that include their prepolitical careers and positions held in the assembly. This latter information – committees sat on, positions held, and electoral history – is useful for constituents and interest groups outside the riding who may need an ally in the legislature.

Constituency Work

The ineffective use of the web points to an inefficiency in terms of both resources and people. Good MP websites can quickly help constituents or direct them to information. Many such sites exist. Carolyn Bennett, a Toronto Liberal MP, and Manitoba MPs Bill Blaikie (NDP) and Reg Alcock (Liberal) are examples of members whose websites provide excellent links to government services and information. These sites allow citizens to access government without physically visiting a member's office. The sites are largely free of partisan political debate and are geared primarily to helping citizens.

Other MPs have more political websites. Given that the House of Commons does not support individual websites there is nothing wrong with this. But this use may have made the Commons hesitant to support MPs in using the web. A more consistent system of sites linked to Parliament might be an effective means of responsiveness to and representation of voters. Without uniform addresses for MPs' websites or links to them from the Parliament of Canada's website, finding individual sites is difficult (Jansen and Thomas 2003). Members should have consistent web addresses, just as they have uniform e-mail addresses. Although this would naturally require a closer monitoring of content, it would eventually result in a greater level of constituency service.

When Responsibilities Overlap

Among other areas of responsibility, provincial governments in Canada deal directly with the largest social policy fields, including health care, education, and social assistance. In addition, provinces have jurisdiction over municipalities and share responsibility with the federal government for the environment and agriculture. The federal government has jurisdiction over monetary policy, immigration, customs, defence, and other national policy fields. The federal government also spends money and funds programs in the fields of health, education, and social services. The result is a rather overlapping patchwork of policy jurisdictions.

In an ideal world, Canadians who encountered problems with a government program, or who were seeking access to a program, would know the appropriate elected official to contact for assistance. Given the often complex web of policy fields and government programs that exists, Canadians can be forgiven for contacting the wrong representative. Determining how often this occurs is difficult, but the surveys of MLAs and MPs shed some light on the frequency of mistaken jurisdictions. Over four-fifths (81 percent) of federal members and two-thirds (68 percent) of provincial legislators surveyed were often approached for assistance by a constituent for a matter that lies outside their jurisdiction.

We can read two things into this finding. First, Canadians are not likely to contact one level of government over another. While federal members are more likely to be contacted on a provincial issue than are provincial members for federal matters, the differences are not huge. Second, members in both jurisdictions are given frequent opportunities to engage in competitive constituency work. After all, a voter who does not know he is knocking at the wrong door for help should be pleased with whoever helps him. Thus should a voter approach an MP over a strictly provincial matter that the federal member can solve, there should be some benefit in doing so.

Table 4.4 illustrates a rather eerie consistency between federal and provincial legislators in handling issues outside their domain. Most MPs and MLAs either always or often forwarded an issue to the appropriate representative. Yet almost 15 percent of each cohort seemed somewhat reticent to do so. Only a very small minority (less than 4 percent) never passed along the concern to the appropriate elected official, but another 10 percent sometimes didn't bother to hand the case over. What did they do with the issue? As Table 4.5 shows, about that same percentage regularly tried first to solve the problem themselves. In fact, there is a great overlap between the "never" cohort in the two tables. A qualitative assessment suggests that these individuals are not necessarily trying to steal credit at the expense of a speedy resolution of a voter's concern.

Table 4.4

Handling of problems outside jurisdiction

How often forward issues to the appropriate level	Federal members forward to provincial MLA (%)	Provincial members forward to federal MP (%)
Always	37.6	45.7
Often	47.1	38.6
Sometimes	11.8	13.6
Never	3.5	2.2
Total (N)	100.0 (85)	100.0 (184)

Sources: Author's surveys of MPs, 2001, and MLAs, 2002.

Table 4.5

Solving problems outside jurisdiction

Initially tries to solve problem through own constituency office	MP tries to solve provincial problem (%)	MLA tries to solve federal problem (%)
Always	10.1	11.5
Often	27.8	27.9
Sometimes	50.6	50.9
Never	11.4	9.7
Total (N)	100.0 (79)	100.0 (165)

Sources: Author's surveys of MPs, 2001, and MLAs, 2002.

In interviews in 2001 and 2002, some members of Parliament mentioned that an initial attempt at solving a provincial problem can be quicker than routing the constituent through the proper channels. One member said, "I have parts of four [provincial ridings] in my district. If it is simply passing along information we know, such as where an office is, it is quicker for us to do it." In the words of a second member, "My constituency staff know most of the big provincial programs and offices. We answer questions but would never open a file." Still others suggested that they have picked up the slack when other elected officials do not provide good service. One member said there was a retiring provincial MLA whose riding overlapped hers. The retiring MLA was slowing down and the MP felt it necessary to step in: "I wouldn't do it otherwise, but if the alternative is a person who is going without help, it is a pretty easy decision."

Finally, it is worth noting that partisan considerations rarely enter the equation when members decide whether to assist Canadians with problems that lie outside their domain. Federal members are no less likely to cooperate with provincial members of a different party than with those who share a partisan or ideological stripe. The same is true of provincial members. In fact, many members commented on the good working relationship between federal and provincial constituency offices. Like a lot of simple constituency work, this cooperation between offices is done without going through the member.

Interestingly, members in Canada, both provincial and federal, rarely use the opportunity to step outside the boundaries of their roles as official elected representatives. Based on qualitative interview evidence in Britain in 2001, elected members there sometimes redirect constituency work to unelected party members in the appropriate jurisdiction. So for example, a Scottish MP might hand off work to a same-party nominee (not member) for the Scottish Parliament rather than a Scottish Parliament member from a different party. The surveys of federal and provincial members in Canada found no such practices.

In sum, it appears that where members overstep their jurisdictions, they do so in responding to constituents. Such responsiveness should be applauded. Members are representing Canadians. Nonetheless, they have a limited amount of time. Spending more effort on representation comes at the cost of their scrutiny and legislative functions. When members are doing a great job at home, they may be neglecting their capital-based duties.

Allocation of Capital Staff

Thus far it is clear that within the riding, members and their staffs are very responsive to their constituents. Whether one-on-one assistance, working with groups, or simply staying in touch, members devote a great deal of time and effort to local work. Further, federal members and provincial and territorial representatives with constituency staff dedicate almost all of their local resources to local services. A legislator's riding staff might be involved in policy, scrutiny, or legislative work, but only as it relates to the riding. As one member said, "My constituency staff are very good at letting people [constituents] know what I am doing in Ottawa and what kinds of programs we can help them with ... They do not engage in the same types of research as my Ottawa staff though" (interview, June 2001). All of a constituency staff's time is spent in constituency-related representational activities, though these can overlap with Ottawa duties.

In the capital, however, the converse is not true: all staffers' attention is less likely to be on a member's legislative and scrutiny functions. While the professionalization of members of Parliament has changed the office and style of service dramatically, the process remains largely unchanged. If an issue cannot be resolved within the riding it is dealt with in the capital. Thus Ottawa-based staffs delegate some of their time to constituency functions. Further, even with a good constituency staff, a member spends a great deal of his or her Ottawa time on constituency matters. Some members may wish to downplay their legislative and scrutiny functions when they are in the riding, but almost without exception, members play up their constituency representational function while in Ottawa.

How much time do elected representatives spend on constituency matters when they are in the legislative environment? As Table 4.6 indicates, about one-third of a member's working day is spent on constituency issues. And capital-based staff, both provincially and federally, spend even more time on local representation and responsiveness. The difference between provincial and federal members is minimal, though there does seem to be some regional variation. As a group, MLAs from Alberta, Saskatchewan, and Manitoba spend the least amount of time (less than 30 percent) on constituency work. By contrast MLAs in the east seem to spend more time on local work. In Newfoundland and Labrador members of the House of Assembly spend an average of 55 percent of their working time on this task. In the other three Atlantic provinces the average time spent on constituency work hovers around 40 percent.

Table 4.6

Allocation of time by members and staff

	Constituency (%)	Policy/legislative (%)
Federal members	35.10	52.80
Ottawa staff	36.40	64.60
Provincial members	37.32	49.10
Provincial capital staff	43.39	54.57

Note: Time for members does not add to 100 percent as other types of work are not included in this table.
Sources: Author's surveys of MPs, 2001, and MLAs, 2002.

At least part of the explanation for this differential lies in the amount of constituency support given to members. The capital staff of Ontario and Quebec MLAs spend only around 35 percent of their time on constituency matters, because the MLAs have constituency staff to handle many of these issues. In jurisdictions with fewer staff resources, it is hardly surprising that staff in the capital spend more of their day helping voters. In addition, much of the "keeping in touch" type of constituency work, including householders, mass mailings, and targeted letters, is produced in the capital. Obviously this consumes at least part of the capital staff's working day, though another sizable chunk of their time still relates to local representation and responsiveness functions. However, capital staff do concentrate the majority of their energy on legislation and scrutiny.

We can draw two tentative conclusions from these data. First, the member as local ombudsperson continues to be a primary function of legislators. Most constituency activity is demand driven. With the possible exception of householders and other mailings, capital staff are not drumming up business but responding to demands that emanate from the constituency. Second, in terms of resources, time is a zero-sum element. Every hour spent on a constituency matter is an hour not spent on legislation and scrutiny functions. Serving constituents is a noble role, but it comes at the expense of other duties. More resources at the local level might alleviate the need for capital staff to engage in riding work, thus freeing them up for policy and legislative research.

Conclusion

The resources provided to members of Parliament for local constituency work have substantially increased in the past four decades.
The days of sitting at a kitchen table on a Saturday hearing from constituents are gone. They have yet to be fully replaced by such high-tech
approaches as providing web-based guidance on how to petition the
government. But the ability of members to respond rapidly and effectively to constituents has been assisted greatly by the physical, financial, and human resources that are now placed at the disposal of MPs
and many MLAs.

In terms of local responsiveness, Canadians are well served. Members dedicate a great deal of their own time and effort to this function,
as well as a large portion of their office resources. Though there is no
empirical evidence, it might be that good service creates its own problems, as members' responsiveness may bring about higher demand.
Survey evidence indicates that members approach their local duties
with a high degree of altruism. There is very little "poaching" on other
members' territory, particularly when it comes to other jurisdictions.
The federal-provincial scrapping that takes place at the first minister
level seems relatively absent from the local scene. When a federal
member does the work of a provincial legislator, or vice versa, it is
probably a matter of either speed or necessity. Further, only marginal
evidence suggests that partisan politics comes into play when matters
of jurisdiction are involved. A federal member is only slightly more
likely to engage in provincial work when the MLA involved is a member
of a different party.

What are the concerns when it comes to local responsiveness?
Three areas could be improved. First, the physical size of some national
ridings is problematic. Despite the introduction of regular constituency weeks, most MPs make weekly return trips to their district.
For many members this trip is arduous, and within the riding many
rural and northern members have a weekend full of driving (or flying)
to look forward to.

Second, members have yet to make full use of information technology, in part because some assemblies see websites as potential partisan traps. Yet web-based technology is an efficient way to overcome many of the problems of space and time. More thought must be put into allowing members to use the web as a legitimate constituency tool. Governments currently spend some time and effort insuring that members do not use their publicly financed mail allowances to spread overtly partisan messages. The same principles and practices could be put in place for websites. Federal and provincial governments all employ websites as part of their citizen outreach. The nonpartisan nature of some of these sites is at best debatable, but nonetheless they provide citizen access to the government. MPs and MLAs can use similar technology to help their constituents understand the maze of government programs and policies. Many members already do this very effectively. More members should be encouraged to do likewise and should be supported by an assembly that recognizes the value of such services. In addition, uniform URLs would allow more convenient citizen access.

Third, members often spend so much time and energy on district matters that they fail to properly fulfill their other duties. Placing too great a share of staff resources at the local level means that important scrutiny and legislative functions run the risk of being given short shrift. As the following chapters indicate, these functions have their own problems and challenges. While members deserve credit for paying attention to local matters, they too often do so at the expense of other responsibilities.

Chapter 4

Strengths

- When it comes to local representation and constituency problem solving, Canadians are well served by their federal and provincial elected officials.

- Most jurisdictions provide legislators with staff and financial resources both in the capital and in the constituency.

- Although the public may be confused about which policy area is federal and which is provincial, there is little overt competition among members to "poach" work from elected officials at different levels. Provincial members engage in federal work (and vice versa) only when it is a minor matter or they believe the constituent would not receive help otherwise.

Weaknesses

- Canadian legislators are not as advanced as elected officials in other countries when it comes to using e-mail and websites efficiently and effectively.

- Travel between the capital and some distant constituencies consumes a considerable portion of a legislator's time. Travel within larger ridings can be almost as time consuming.

5 OPPORTUNITIES IN THE ASSEMBLY

The ability of members of legislatures to perform their duties is a function of the participatory nature of legislatures. This chapter focuses on some of the features of parliamentary government that provide participatory opportunities for members. Question period allows them to scrutinize the government, members' statements allow them to represent broader interests, and private members' business allows them to initiate legislation and debate. Such measures of participation inside an assembly are just as crucial as who is elected to serve in office, the measure of participation discussed in Chapter 2.

We can assess the democratic strength of an assembly by the openness of its rules. Rules, both formal and informal, allow members more or less opportunity to participate fully in scrutiny functions. For examples, the rules surrounding question period, and the culture that exists around a particular assembly's practice in question period, can favour questions from party leaders over those from critics. Alternatively, these rules can encourage many members to hold the government to account through oral questions. But rules alone are not enough. Members must also be willing to take advantage of opportunities both to scrutinize and to represent. If members bypass these opportunities, or use them to further purely partisan ends, the best rules are essentially impotent.

In addition, parliaments should be forums where members can place alternative policy positions, and alternative governments, in front of the public. We cannot criticize any parliamentary activity simply because it is overtly partisan. Westminster parliaments are organized around parties and designed to be arenas of debate that thrive on conflict (Rush 2001, 9-11). However, opportunities to represent broader interests are squandered if they are used only to sell a party position. Moreover, parliamentary reform, particularly reform aimed at improving the opportunities for participation of backbench members, will quickly die if all backbenchers cannot put aside partisan differences and focus on institutional development. Members must use the opportunities they have under the rules of their assembly to put forth constructive debate and policy alternatives.

Question Period

Question period is without doubt the most watched event of the legislative day, and the period that garners the most media coverage and therefore public attention. To say that some theatre is involved in question period is an understatement, but to suggest that the importance of question period is highly overrated is folly. The infamy of question period, however, is not difficult to understand, given that insults are hurled across the floor of the legislative arena. Question period thrives on confrontation, demands members to be at their (supposed) angriest, and levels the playing field between opposition MPs and ministers of the Crown. There is little restriction (beyond language) on the type of question that members can raise, or on the answers given. For members, question period is the most open and accessible method of accountability in the legislative arena (Docherty 1999, 40).

The free-flowing nature of question period includes the always-present threat that a minister of the Crown might be caught out on a matter of impropriety or simply unaware of activities within her or his domain. It is the one period of the legislative day when opposition parties can effectively hijack the agenda of the government. Properly orchestrated, question period can force a prime minister into reversing policy decisions or, the ultimate penalty, seeking the resignation of a cabinet minister.

Question period is not without its problems. The very act of scrutiny, which demands tough questions of government activities and cabinet ministers, contains the potential to bring the entire legislative process into public disrepute. Though the norms and standards of Parliament do not allow members to impugn the honesty of other members, this is the only real restriction placed on legislators within the chamber. This restriction holds for all legislative proceedings, not just question period, but the rule is most frequently breached during the thrust and parry of the question period debate. Yet the seemingly arcane rules of privilege that dictate that all members are honourable, and thus cannot be accused of deceitfulness, also allow members to escape civil sanctions for statements uttered inside the chamber (Marleau and Montpetit 2000, 71-2). Hence, while sitting legislators cannot question the honesty of their colleagues, they can accuse any other Canadian of the most heinous behaviour imaginable without fear of legal sanctions. Again, while all speech in the legislature and its committees is protected, such accusations are more likely during question period.

The rationale for such a rule was to provide members of legislatures with a shield against external threats (ibid., 53-4). Proper scrutiny demands that members be free to question the government on any matter within its jurisdiction. Equally, if members are to represent constituents or any citizens, they must be able to debate freely. The threat of a lawsuit, real or imagined, can stifle important democratic debate.

Yet members can use this protection as a club rather than a shield. In one recent provincial case that gained national attention, Ontario Progressive Conservative Garry Guzzo threatened to use a question to the solicitor general to name individuals who had been under investigation for alleged sexual offences involving minors (Mackie 2001; Boyle 2001). Because no charges had been laid, the names of the people had never been published. Had Guzzo mentioned their names outside the legislature, he could have been subject to slander and contempt of court charges; inside, he was protected by parliamentary privilege. He eventually backed down on his threat (Thompson 2001). The damage caused to all members, though difficult to measure, was nonetheless evident. Instead of being an arena where members speak up for individuals, the legislature can too easily become a bully pulpit. Members must be very careful in choosing to take advantage of the protections afforded them.

Even when members do not abuse the privilege of privilege, question period can bring out the best and worst of the scrutiny function. In many ways question period is a Catch-22 of legislative scrutiny. It works best when members are at their angriest, tough lines are drawn between government and opposition, and the debate often turns personal. Simply put, Parliament looks worst when it is at its most effective. The most obvious example of this occurs when ministers are being grilled for inappropriate behaviour within their departments. When troubles arise within a department, or a minister is taken to task for questionable departmental spending, the dirty laundry is usually aired during question period. This can stall a government's ability to move on with its own agenda. Instead, the Prime Minister's Office is compelled to engage in damage control and weigh the costs and benefits of sticking with a minister or seeking his or her resignation.

In 2002 two major embarrassments for the federal government were played out during question period. In the first, two ministers of the Crown were forced to step down. Defence Minister Art Eggleton was accused of providing a former girlfriend with a government contract that had not gone through the tendering process (Scoffield 2002; Laghi 2002b). At approximately the same time, Public Works Minister Don Boudria was under fire for lodging at a resort owned by a company doing business with the government (Leblanc 2002). The efforts of the opposition, combined with the fact that Eggleton was an MP from Liberal-rich Toronto, made his departure a foregone conclusion; he was easy to replace. Boudria's exit was harder. A staunch ally of the prime minister, the former "Rat Pack" member was being accused of the same type of political folly that he had condemned during the Mulroney years (ibid.). Chrétien was much more loyal to one of his key cabinet colleagues; though Boudria left his Public Works spot in late May 2002, he kept his House leader's position.

The government faced similar controversy when Solicitor General Lawrence MacAulay was accused of improper tendering of government grants to companies and organizations in his home province of Prince Edward Island, including some educational institutions associated with family members (McCarthy 2002a; also Atkinson and Docherty 2004). Eventually MacAulay was replaced as solicitor general by another Prince Edward Island Liberal, Wayne Easter. Easter lasted in this post for just over a year and was not part of Martin's first cabinet. Another PEI MP, Joe McGuire, was tapped for a cabinet spot, as minister of the Atlantic Canada Opportunities Agency. In a period of a little over a year, three of four (or 75 percent) of the PEI cohort of MPs had served some time in cabinet.

In each of these cases, the constant glare of media and the continual questioning of opposition MPs crippled the government's pursuit of its own agenda. Issues such as health care, the Kyoto Protocol, and plans to address Aboriginal concerns, all part of Prime Minister Chrétien's self-defined legacy project, were knocked off the front pages by questions of government ethics. The only thing the government could do to regain control was sacrifice cabinet ministers.

Yet this outcome highlights the dangerous and almost contradictory nature of question period and the scrutiny function. In such instances the competence and integrity of the government is questioned. Opposition parties are merely performing their duties (though they no doubt relish the smell of blood when a minister appears vulnerable). When negligent ministers are rousted from their cabinet seats, it is the tangible evidence that the scrutiny function works. But this also makes all politicians and therefore Parliament appear less than honourable. Unfortunately it allows Canadians to assume incorrectly that all politicians are self-serving.

Question period is the most open display of scrutiny. Part of the strength of question period in Canada is its unscripted nature. Unlike Westminster, where most questions are given to the government in writing before being raised in the Commons, members in all Canadian legislatures can spring questions on cabinet ministers unannounced. Canadian assemblies also provide for written questions, which when tabled in the legislature require some response, usually within a specified period of approximately two weeks. The questions and answers are published in the proceedings of the legislature. In many ways, written questions are the precursor to freedom of information inquiries by members of the public.

The broad rules governing question period are covered in the standing orders (or rules of proceedings) of each legislature. The title "question period" reflects the only requirement of this part of the routine proceedings. Members are required to put a question through the speaker to a minister of the Crown. However, the minister is not required to answer the question. In fact in some jurisdictions (Ontario, for example) the standing orders or rules of the assembly specifically state that answers are not required. Consequently members cannot ask the speaker to force a minister to address an issue. This rule allows ministers to sidestep potential land mines, though avoiding a question comes with its own dubious distinction. Most question periods occur daily, or are part of the routine proceedings of the day. In most assemblies, question period follows members' statements and ministerial statements, but precedes debate on legislation or motions. In addition, most assemblies allow parliamentary secretaries to respond when a minister is absent and do not allow ministers to question each other. Beyond these standard practices, there is much variation in both the attention given question period and the culture that surrounds it within each assembly. Table 5.1 outlines some of these differences.

Perhaps the most notable variation is the time devoted to question period. From a daily fifteen minutes in British Columbia to one hour a day in Ontario, the time allotted question period suggests a range of opportunities for members to participate. More questions can be posed in one hour than in fifteen minutes. In a typical week that the legislature sits in Nova Scotia, three and a half hours are available for questioning the government, compared to an hour and a quarter in British

Table 5.1

Question period in Canadian legislatures

Jurisdiction	Length of question period	Limit on supplementary questions	Number of people asking questions	Do government private members routinely ask questions?
House of Commons	45 minutes daily	Yes	15-18	Yes
Newfoundland and Labrador	30 minutes daily	No	3-4	No
Prince Edward Island	40 minutes daily	Yes	1	No
Nova Scotia	60 minutes Tuesday and Thursday, 90 minutes on Wednesday	No	10-11 in one hour	No
New Brunswick	30 minutes daily	No	5-6	Yes
Quebec	45 minutes daily	No	7-8	Yes
Ontario	60 minutes daily	No	13-15	Yes
Manitoba	40 minutes daily	Yes	10-13	Yes
Saskatchewan	25 minutes daily	No	4-5	No
Alberta	50 minutes daily	Yes	10-12	Yes
British Columbia	15 minutes daily	Yes	4-5	Yes
Yukon	30 minutes daily	No	7-8	No
NWT	60 minutes daily	Yes	4-5	No parties
Nunavut	60 minutes daily	Yes	7-9	No parties

Sources: Legislative websites; Hansards; standing orders. Information on the number of different questioners taken from a survey of Hansards in each of the assemblies for the fall 2002 sittings.

Columbia. In addition, long preambles to questions (and answers) eat into the time available for questions. Different legislatures have adopted different customs for asking and answering questions. Ontario is known for long questions and answers, and as a result its sixty-minute question period barely provides for more questions (and questioners) than Manitoba's forty-minute period. Seven or eight questions can be asked and answered in the Yukon within a half-hour, about the same as are addressed in double the time in Nunavut.

Time is not the only impediment to full participation. Assemblies that focus most of their question period on leaders' questions may not provide much opportunity for critics to hold ministers to account. The use of supplementary questions tends to reinforce leader questions at the expense of private members. On the plus side, supplementary questions are follow-ups to a minister's response and allow further discussion of government action or inaction. It is scrutiny in its most unscripted form.

Additionally, while private members on the government side of the House play an effective role in accountability and scrutiny, they rarely exercise these functions in the open forum of question period. And every question asked by a government private member denies the opportunity for a question from the opposition benches (see Chapter 6 for further discussion). With the exception of the non-party-based assemblies in the Northwest Territories and Nunavut, questions rotate between parties, beginning with the leader of the official Opposition and followed by any other opposition leaders. Usually more supplementary questions are given to party leaders than to private members.

The problem of participation is further heightened in assemblies with multiple opposition parties. The most dramatic example is the House of Commons, where up to four opposition parties (along with government private members) have shared forty-five minutes each day to question the government openly. During the thirty-fifth Parliament (1993-7) only two opposition parties had recognized status in the Commons. In the thirty-sixth Parliament, when both the New Democrats and Progressive Conservatives had regained recognized party status, the problem became more serious (Docherty 1998). Specifically, the New Democrats and Progressive Conservatives feared they would be shut out of question period if the existing question format were retained. In previous Parliaments, the first few questions (and accompanying supplementaries) were conventionally considered leader's questions. Given the long preambles and responses that were customary in the House, members of the fourth and fifth parties were legitimately concerned that their leaders and members would have little, if any, time for questions.

Negotiations among the House leaders of the five parties established a new formula for asking questions. The questions would begin with a complete rotation of the opposition parties. Then the Alliance and Bloc would each have two questions in turn, followed by a Liberal backbench question. The five-party rotation would then follow until the forty-five minutes were up. In order for this to work, much shorter questions and answers would be necessary. The solution was the enforcement of a new "thirty-second rule," under which questioners would have fifteen seconds to pose a question, and ministers would have thirty seconds to respond. The new formula for question period was adopted when the thirty-sixth Parliament first met in September 1997 (Docherty 1998).

The alterations in procedure between the thirty-fifth and thirty-sixth Parliaments of Canada provide a good example of how changes in rules can affect participation. In the thirty-fifth Parliament, the lack of official party status cost the New Democrats and Progressive Conservatives the opportunity to consistently participate in question period. Their ability to participate was left in the hands of the speaker, who might or might not choose to recognize members from these parties. After the House leaders reached their agreement, a more orderly process was put into practice.

The change in informal rules, coupled with the agreement of the speaker to enforce a stricter time limit on questions, produced a marked increase in the number of questions asked during question period without increasing the time allocated to this scrutiny function. The actual number of questions asked increased by over 50 percent. In November 1996, an average of 14.8 different questions were put forth during question time. This increased to 23.8 questions in November 1997 (Docherty 1998). The net beneficiaries of this change have been the fourth and fifth parties (the New Democrats and Progressive Conservatives in both the thirty-sixth and thirty-seventh Parliaments). They have gone from asking less than one question per day to being regular contributors. There has even been an increase in the number of questions posed by government backbenchers, but it is too soon to measure the impact of the new four-party Parliament on how many questions they ask.

While there is little evidence that this change has substantially increased scrutiny, it has produced a marked improvement in participation. More questions mean more questioners. The fact that question periods in Ottawa typically see from fifteen to eighteen different people ask questions indicates a stronger participation rate than was the case before 1997, when the range was typically between nine and twelve. Leaders still dominate question period, but private members have an increased opportunity to enter the arena of accusation and response. Of course more questions also mean more answers. In 1996, a typical question period would see questions asked of nine different ministers. The next year, this increased to nearly thirteen different ministers (Docherty 1998). On days when a particular issue dominates, one or two cabinet ministers can bear the brunt of many questions. On days when numerous issues are on the public agenda, opposition parties can cast their scrutiny nets farther from shore in hopes of catching a minister ill prepared. The result is less domination by the opposition front bench and an opportunity for cabinet critics to demonstrate their own talents.

Members' Statements

Another vehicle for responsiveness and participation is the ability of elected officials to make statements in the legislative chamber about issues that are particularly important to constituents, citizens, or particular demographic segments of Canadians. While most of the routine orders and proceedings of legislatures deal specifically with legislation or the government's agenda, two areas give members more freedom deal with issues that are important to them, namely private members' bills (discussed in the next section) and members' statements.

Members' statements originated in the House of Commons, though the advent of a distinct period for members' statements is a product both of evolution and conscious parliamentary reform. Officially, members' statements became part of the routine proceedings and orders of the day in the fall of 1982, but this change only made easier and institutionalized what had been occurring for years, namely MPs addressing the House on matters usually of local, or occasionally of regional or national, importance. Like most changes in Canadian legislatures, these practices in the federal House were eventually adopted in most provincial assemblies.

Between 1867 and 1927, MPs needed the unanimous consent of the chamber if they wished to speak on a matter that did not appear on the order paper. This provision was relaxed in 1927 to give members more flexibility to speak, but only when it was of "urgent and pressing necessity." Of course urgency was very much in the mind of the person speaking, and in 1968 the House and speaker began clamping down on the practice of members speaking on local and less timely issues (Marleau and Montpetit 2000). Between 1975 and 1982 the opportunity for members to speak was quite popular and limited to private members. The power to address the House was provided under Standing Order 43 (the urgent and necessary provision). In November 1982 the Special Committee on Standing Orders and Procedures (known informally as the Lefebvre Committee after its chair, Tom Lefebvre) tabled its forty-one-page third report. The report claimed that Standing Order 43 was very rarely used for its original purpose of "making a motion without notice in a genuine case of urgent and pressing necessity" (House of Commons 1982, 17-19). Lefebvre suggested replacing Standing Order 43 with a new rule that more accurately reflected the practice of members.

The result was Standing Order 31, which provides members with very broad discretion in the types of statements they can make. Members are not allowed to attack other members, senators, the Senate, or private citizens, nor are they allowed to denounce specific court rulings. The restrictions against reading verse, greetings, or congratulations are roundly ignored by most members and recent speakers (Marleau and Montpetit 2000, 363). The standing orders do not allow cabinet ministers to make members' statements; all other members are allowed to participate.

This restriction, and the broad latitude provided members in terms of content, recognize that private members in particular have limited opportunity and resources to focus attention on specific issues. By contrast, members of the executive have a plethora of public platforms and a wealth of resources with which to draw national attention to their pet concerns. While not necessarily planned, then, the spirit of the standing order and its subsequent interpretation has allowed members some leeway in their ability to represent particular groups. For example, nothing prevents members from discussing a policy issue that does not fall within their critic portfolio. Nor is a member from Ontario prohibited from discussing the plight of the east coast fishery.

Unlike the now-extinct practice of pounding on desks, members' statements are not a uniquely Canadian phenomenon. Other jurisdictions with a Westminster parliamentary system have similar opportunities for private members. Members' statements in the Australian House of Representatives almost mirror the structure of the Canadian Commons. Fifteen minutes is allocated, as in Canada, though Australia has stuck to a time limit of ninety seconds per speaker while Canada shortened its time to sixty seconds in 1986. Ministers in Australia are prevented from participating, and the subjects range from the most local to the broadest of international concerns. Interestingly, Australia specifically includes members' statements in its website list of "Opportunities for Private Members" (Australia 2002). Neither the United Kingdom, with its much larger House of Commons, nor New Zealand, with a mixed House of single-member districts and proportionally elected members, provides an opportunity for members to address the chamber, and through it the nation, in this manner.

Many provincial and territorial assemblies permit some form of members' statement, the exceptions being Nova Scotia, Quebec, and the Yukon (see Table 5.2). The members' statement period in Newfoundland and Labrador lasts less than half as long as in Ottawa (six minutes as opposed to fifteen) and members are prohibited from commenting on government policy. This restriction effectively limits members to statements of congratulations or greetings, though many opposition members do use this time to comment on the "lack of government action" in certain policy fields. Alberta provides eight minutes but only two days a week. Saskatchewan allows ministers to participate in its daily statement period, but they are not allowed "to remark on matters

Table 5.2

Members' statements in Canadian legislatures

Jurisdiction	Time allocated to members' statements	Time limits on statements
House of Commons	15 minutes daily	1 minute
Newfoundland and Labrador	6 minutes daily	1 minute
Prince Edward Island	5 minutes daily	1.5 minutes
Nova Scotia	None	n/a
New Brunswick	10 minutes daily	1 minute
Quebec	None	n/a
Ontario	15 minutes daily	1.5 minutes
Manitoba	10 minutes daily	2 minutes
Saskatchewan	10 minutes daily	1.5 minutes
Alberta	8 minutes twice a week	2 minutes
British Columbia	6 minutes daily	2 minutes
Northwest Territories	One statement per member	2.5 minutes
Nunavut	One statement per member	2.5 minutes
Yukon	None	n/a

Sources: Legislative websites; Hansards; standing orders; author's survey of provincial and territorial legislative clerks, 2002.

relating to government policy or ministerial action" (Saskatchewan 2003).

The sporadic existence of a members' statements period across the country (and indeed in other Westminster national assemblies) suggests that the purpose served by this part of the routine proceedings is not yet clearly understood. The inclusion of ministers in Saskatchewan (as long as they do not comment on ministerial matters) suggests that statements there are to be of a local or at least nonpartisan nature, while limiting the content in Newfoundland renders the statements there less forceful. In the House of Commons, it is not altogether clear yet how members both view and use their statement period. Members use it for many different purposes, which suggests that it should foster individual and not party participation. Yet the fact that members speak in order and that the order is determined by party standings in the House is suggestive of the more traditional party ties in legislative affairs.

Members are beginning to move beyond simple partisan members' statements. Some members use this opportunity to speak to the larger,

Table 5.3

Gender and members' statements

	% of women in Canadian population	% of women in House of Commons	% of statements by women MPs	% of statements about women/ women's issues
35th Parliament	52	18.4	23.7	6.9
36th Parliament	52	20.5	27.4	5.6

Source: House of Commons, *Debates*, various.

nongeographic constituencies they see themselves representing. There is limited evidence that members use this statement period to redress some demographic underrepresentation. A random sampling of members' statements in the falls of 1994, 1995, 1998, and 1999 found some interesting differences in the use of this time. As Table 5.3 indicates, female MPs are in a minority, but they are slightly overrepresented (proportionately) in availing themselves of members' statements. In the thirty-fifth Parliament nearly one-quarter of all statements in the period surveyed were made by women. This increased to over 27 percent in the subsequent Parliament. Interestingly, while more women were making statements in 1998 and 1999, there were fewer statements concerning individual women or policies that might be considered women's issues.

Remembering that the New Democrats and Conservatives were not regular participants in the thirty-fifth Parliament, it is worth noting that over 60 percent of statements about women and women's issues in this Parliament were made by Liberal MPs. Over 15 percent of all women's issues statements in this Parliament were made by the Bloc Québécois. The drop in the number of statements concerning women's issues occurred despite the regular participation of the NDP in the thirty-sixth Parliament. In that Parliament, over 10 percent of all women's issues statements were made by New Democrats, while the percentage by Bloc MPs fell by over 10 percentage points. The amount of time that each party devoted to women's issues may be a reflection of their ideological predispositions. Almost 10 percent of all members' statements made by the NDP were about women's issues, followed by the Liberals at almost 7 percent. The Reform dedicated less than 5 percent of their statements to matters directly concerning women. No Progressive Conservative MPs made statements concerning women's issues in either Parliament.

Members' statements also provide an opportunity for members to make up for a lack of regional representation. If electoral success evades parties in a particular part of the country, they can try to use this free time in the Commons to speak on behalf of regions that are underrepresented in cabinet. Alternatively a party in opposition might have some electoral support in a region but not hold any seats there. Members' statements allow them to try to speak for a region they do not physically represent. This is important in light of the increasingly regionalized character of the House of Commons, particularly after the 1997 and 2000 elections (Carty, Cross, and Young 2000).

It is not always clear whether a member is speaking to a region to enhance his or her party's status in that region, or to inform the government and the country about particular concerns in that area. The data as collected cannot determine the motives of the speaker, and a smattering of both motives doubtless underlies any statement an MP makes. A simple comparison, however, reveals that MPs from some parts of the country are more likely to make regional statements than constituency-type statements.

Table 5.4 compares the region of the member speaking with the focus of the statement, whether constituency, regional, or national in nature. As the table makes clear, statements reflecting the nation (this includes policy issues that are not specifically regional) are the most popular focus of MPs during statement period. With the exception of Quebec MPs in the thirty-sixth Parliament, national statements dominate all regional categories. Additionally, the accepted wisdom in Canada that Ontarians see provincial issues as national ones may well be reflected in the statements of Ontario members. Ontario MPs appear both more national and more local in orientation. In both the thirty-fifth and thirty-sixth Parliaments, the Liberal Party dominated

Table 5.4

Focus of members' statements, by region

Focus of statement	Region of member (%)			
	East	Quebec	Ontario	West
35th Parliament				
Constituency	31.6	11.2	36.7	19.3
Regional	23.7	44.7	3.9	15.2
National	44.7	44.2	59.4	65.6
Number	76.0	197.0	256.0	270.0
36th Parliament				
Constituency	34.6	24.7	42.6	21.7
Regional	26.9	39.0	5.3	22.1
National	38.5	36.3	52.1	56.1
Number	78.0	223.0	284.0	253.0

Source: House of Commons, *Debates*, various.

Ontario. And in both Parliaments, statements of a regional nature were in the overwhelming minority among Ontario MPs.

One of the more interesting discoveries is the increase in the percentage of regional statements coming from both the west and east in the thirty-sixth Parliament. The 1997 election brought about a significant drop in Liberal representation in both regions, with Reform doing significantly better in the west and the New Democrats and Progressive Conservatives rebounding from near obscurity to respectability in the east. The result was a large drop in regional representation in the government caucus. Other parties responded with an increasing number of statements on the record about concerns within these underrepresented regions.

This increasing focus on regional concerns during members' statements mirrors the increasingly regional nature of the House of Commons. The larger proportion of regional statements in the thirty-sixth Parliament did not come at the expense of local concerns but rather of national issues. Those concerned that the Canadian political party system is becoming increasingly narrow and territorial will not find solace in this seeming trend.

Private Members' Business

Question period is a clearly delineated scrutiny function. Members' statements allow members to choose between scrutiny (the criticism of government policy) and representation of voter interests. In both cases opposition members or government private members have the freedom to choose which question they will ask or statement they will make (though their political party will have some say in whether members can participate). A third area allows all members to participate in the legislative function of governing – at least in terms of choosing the topic or initiating debate – namely private members' business, which includes private members' bills and motions.

Every legislature in Canada provides its members some opportunity to initiate legislation. Of course, the type of this legislation, and their ability to push the legislation through the chamber, are very much restricted. As a result the opportunity to participate through private members' bills is somewhat superficial. Members are free to draft and table almost any bill they choose, but they face several major hurdles in attempting to have the bill passed. The scope of private members' bills is limited to legislation that would not see a direct public expenditure or an increase in public taxes. The roots of this limit go back to the founding of parliamentary government, when the Crown, needing money, would seek it from Parliament. The executive, acting on behalf of the Crown, were the only members of Parliament permitted to introduce tax or spend legislation (Deshpande 1995, 24). Members of the Commons outside the executive have to be very careful in creating their legislation, because even indirect or less obvious expenditures can quickly be ruled out of order.

Because members are circumscribed in what they can introduce, they are discouraged from engaging in broader public policy issues. Instead members introduce the "doable," those measures they think will have a greater chance of passing legislative scrutiny. Many of these bills have more symbolic than real value. In the words of one member of Parliament, private members' bills are likely to be concerned with making both "hockey and lacrosse national games and silly things like that" (in Lincoln et al. 2001, 12). On the other hand, when private members' legislation touches on social policy, such as abortion or capital punishment, it can be very controversial.

However, limited scope has not decreased private members' interest in introducing legislation. During the thirty-fifth Parliament the 261 private members introduced 410 pieces of legislation. In the thirty-sixth Parliament, over 600 private members' bills were introduced by the 265 eligible members (Walsh 2002, 31). Only part of this increase was due to "recycled" private members' legislation that had died when the thirty-fifth House dissolved and been reintroduced in the subsequent Parliament (32). Further, these numbers represent only legislation that was actually introduced for first reading. Requests by private members to draft legislation numbered over twice the number of bills that made it to the floor of the chamber for possible debate.

The chances of proceeding with legislation are even more daunting. Getting a bill to first reading is the easiest stage. After a bill is properly drafted, one simply introduces it in the legislature. The next problem is getting the bill debated. While the rules governing the debate and passage of private members' bills vary from jurisdiction to jurisdiction in Canada, such bills all have two things in common: their fate is ultimately controlled by the government, and very few make it through the legislature. One member compared having a bill called for debate to winning the 6/49 lottery: the odds against it are overwhelming and many other ticket holders envy the winner (Lincoln et al. 2001, 12).

This difficulty is despite the fact that most legislatures build private members' time into the legislative calendar. The trouble lies in determining which legislation will be debated. For example, in the Commons, Ontario, and Alberta, private members' bills are chosen for debate by lottery. In some jurisdictions, private members' bills are given more favourable treatment after passage through second reading (and committee if applicable). In New Brunswick and Ontario, for example, private members' bills are treated the same as government bills after the second reading and committee stage. Among other things this means they are carried on the daily orders and notice paper of the legislature. However, the decision to call them for a final reading rests with the government.

Far less time is allotted in the legislative calendar for debating private members' bills. This limit makes some intuitive sense. After all, the main priority for governments is to pass their own legislative agenda, and the rules of assemblies must accommodate this preference. In addition, the scope of private members' bills is far more circumscribed than government bills. As a result there is arguably less detail to be debated, and less need for longer study. Moreover, many private members' bills serve very political (as opposed to legislative) purposes. The fact that private members' legislation is far more limited in breadth than government bills provides greater latitude to members who introduce them. Private members can table all kinds of bills knowing they will never see the legislative light of day. Further, if they were to become law, the responsibility for implementing them would rest with the government and not the members themselves. As a result, members sometimes table legislation that they know is essentially dead upon arrival.

As Table 5.5 indicates, legislative activity varies across jurisdictions. In terms of private members' legislation, the Commons is certainly the busiest assembly. Ontario is the only other jurisdiction where private members' bills are introduced more frequently than government legislation. Other assemblies – the National Assembly in Quebec and Confederation House in Prince Edward Island, for example – see very few private members' bills. The constant is the higher success rate of government bills compared to private members' bills. We note that in the period covered by Table 5.5 most legislatures were controlled by majority governments. It is therefore no great shock that government bills were more likely to pass; any majority government wishing to pass its platform should be able to do so successfully.

More remarkably, the fewer private members' bills introduced, the more likely they are to pass. In Ontario, where an average of eighty-four such bills are introduced each term, less than 6 percent become law. In Quebec and PEI, half of all private members' bills become law, though only four to six are introduced. In the case of Prince Edward

Table 5.5

Success rates of government and private members' legislation, 1997-2002

Jurisdiction	Government bills		Private members' legislation	
	Introduced	Passed	Introduced	Passed
House of Commons (per session)	63	50	298	5
Newfoundland and Labrador	53	49	MHAs introduce resolutions only	
Prince Edward Island	46	43	4	2
Nova Scotia	40	35	20	1
New Brunswick	67	66	3	1
Quebec	85	75	6	3
Ontario	50	39	84	5
Manitoba	54	53	6	2
Saskatchewan	66	66	36	1
Alberta	38	36	25	3
British Columbia	47	45	9	1
NWT	35	34	1	1
Nunavut	15	14	–	–
Yukon	25	24	4	1

Note: Provincial and territorial clerks were asked, "What has been the average number of bills introduced and passed over the past five years?"
Source: Author's survey of provincial and territorial legislative clerks, 2002.

Island, a motion allowing a private member to introduce a bill must be passed before the bill is even introduced (PEI 1998, Standing Order 65(1-5)). This requirement effectively restricts the number of bills tabled, and accounts both for the fewer bills introduced and for their greater success rate.

In sum, private members' bills allow non-cabinet members to participate in the legislative realm. At the same time, the rules prescribing both the content and passage of private members' legislation are such that meaningful participation is more illusion than reality. The inability of members to table "money" bills is a natural function of the Westminster form of parliamentary government. The executive controls the purse strings, and only the executive can be responsible for raising and spending public monies. This maxim could be relaxed and private members could have latitude to introduce more meaningful legislation.

Of course, a government would only be willing to do this if it could exercise even greater control over which private members' legislation would be debated and called for a vote. And herein lies the dilemma, for a government that opened the doors for more meaningful participation from all members would be hypocritical if it then let even more bills die on the order paper. Or bizarrely, perhaps the government would be forced to draw a whip on its own backbench on a matter belonging to private members. Increasing the scope of private members' bills might broaden the scope of what is considered matters of confidence. As it stands now, private members' bills are more chimera than meaningful vehicle for participation. Yet changes to make the mirage real are unlikely and even of questionable value. In the end, governments must necessarily control the legislation they will be faced with implementing.

Conclusion

Whether it is through question period, members' statements, or the introduction of private members' legislation, each legislature in Canada provides its members varying degrees of opportunity to participate in scrutiny, representation, and legislative functions. For members, the struggle is often one of balancing competing interests, namely the need to keep the government accountable for its actions and the need to engage in proactive policy work. Different parts of the legislative calendar provide occasions for each of these functions.

Question period is clearly the focal point of the legislative day. It allows members to shine and has the capacity to bring a government's legislative agenda to a complete halt. When used correctly, it is the very essence of parliamentary scrutiny. Question period is a very public opportunity for opposition members (and government members) to call into question government action, inaction, and mis-action. In Canada, the unique and healthy post-question period scrum adds the prospect of direct interaction between members of the media and members of Parliament. Not only does this provide a healthy context to the debate in question period but it also allows many opposition backbenchers the promise of demonstrating their talents to the country.

The potential Catch-22 of question period is that when it works best, it tends to show Parliament and parliamentarians in the worst light. A resigning cabinet minister, unable to withstand the question period spotlight, should serve as the symbol of the success of the accountability function of Parliament. Instead, such resignations all too often suggest that politicians are incompetent, corrupt, or at best out to get each other no matter what the cost. Members are often complicit in this impression, when question period seems less about questions and answers and more about insults and personal vitriol. It does not help when some members use parliamentary privilege to attack citizens without fear of legal ramifications.

Finally, question period is too often used to highlight leader strengths and weaknesses rather than the talents of individual members. As our analysis of the federal question time indicated, the lion's share of time is given over to opposition leaders. While this does not necessarily detract from the scrutiny function – and indeed can help to highlight it – dominance by leaders does come at a price. Many talented members are left out of the question period loop, as this part of the legislative timetable inevitably reinforces leaders and diminishes the role of private members.

By contrast, members' statements are given over almost exclusively to private members. Federally, members have used the time to address issues from the most serious (such as AIDS) to the most local (municipal celebrations of Groundhog Day). While the latter are hardly matters of national importance, their recognition in the House of Commons is a tradition that does play a role in local boosterism. Larger issues tend to dominate members' statements, however, and our cursory examination of them points to some interesting patterns. Women MPs have made up, at least partially, for their lower numbers in the House by making more than their share of statements, though these statements do not all relate to women's issues. Members' statements have also responded to the lack of government representation in the regions. During the thirty-sixth Parliament, when the government had no representation in Nova Scotia and little in the rest of the Atlantic region (or in the West), members of the opposition parties used this time to bring matters of regional importance to the attention of the government. Members from regions that the government dominated were far more inclined to talk of local or parochial issues.

In terms of legislation, the use of private members' bills varies across the country. Private members' legislation rarely has a dramatic impact inside assemblies, and is often fruitless and discouraging. Nonetheless, it does allow private members to initiate public policy within the assembly. Thus it is a proactive tool for legislators. Many federal MPs use the mechanism, though few find success. The trick for both governments and private members is to provide more freedom for private members' legislation without compromising the government's control over its own agenda. To date, no jurisdiction in Canada has done this successfully.

CHAPTER 5

Strengths

✦ Question period works best when opposition members force cabinet ministers to be accountable for administrative or policy shortcomings.

✦ Changes to the structure of question period in the House of Commons after the 1997 election have resulted in more questions and more MPs asking questions. This has improved scrutiny and participation.

✦ The unscripted nature of question period allows for true accountability. Cabinet ministers must be aware of the activities in their department and Opposition members must be confident of the questions they ask.

✦ Members' statements provide additional opportunities for participation in the assembly. At their best they make up for a lack of regional or demographic representation in the chamber.

Weaknesses

✦ When legislators put too much theatre and too little substance into question period, the legislature appears at its least professional and can turn the public off the political process.

✦ When used simply for partisan purpose, members' statements reinforce politics over responsiveness and representation.

✦ The success of private members' business (and in particular private members' bills) is mixed. It can provide a forum for legislative participation by members outside cabinet. Yet so few such bills become law that truly meaningful participation is often more illusion than reality.

6

SCRUTINY AND THE SIZE OF LEGISLATURES

On 1 October 1996, Premier Mike Harris stood outside the steps of Queen's Park in Toronto. In front of him, and behind the reporters and onlookers, was a large flatbed truck with twenty-seven chairs, each representing a chair and desk that would normally be in the legislative assembly. The photo opportunity was well staged and beautifully executed, and made exactly the point that the premier hoped it would. In introducing the Fewer Politicians Act, Harris was not simply fulfilling an election promise. He was making a statement about the role of politicians and public attitudes toward them: there are too many politicians. Politicians spend public monies, both through legislation (the introduction of programs that cost money) and in basic government overhead (salaries, staff, office space). In this view, if we want to save money, one of the most efficient ways to do it is to reduce the number of politicians. The premier further suggested that the number of Ontario MPPs be determined by its federal ridings. Instead of paying for the redistribution, Ontario would simply use the federal boundaries.

While it might have been politically brilliant, the move to reduce the size of the Ontario legislature represents a complete misinterpretation of the role of members of assemblies in parliamentary settings. Politicians in some jurisdictions may spend money, but in Westminster systems they do not. Executives do. Members of Parliament are charged with keeping the executive honest. This is their scrutiny and accountability function. In reducing the size of the Ontario Legislative Assembly, Premier Harris did not simply reduce some expenditures; rather he reduced the capacity of the assembly to perform its scrutiny function, thereby reducing the checks on the authority of his and successive cabinets.

Perhaps the most disturbing thing about the actions of the former Ontario premier is that they were not unique in Canada. Since 1990, five provinces have reduced the number of seats in their assemblies. The reductions have ranged from a low of 5 percent in New Brunswick to Ontario's high of 20 percent. Only the federal government and British Columbia have increased the size of their elected assemblies in the same period.

This chapter examines the ability of members to properly participate in such scrutiny responsibilities as question period and committee work, and the problems that small assemblies face in allowing members to do their job. The institutional problem of scrutiny and legislative size is exacerbated when multiple parties hold seats, or a governing party enjoys an overwhelming majority. Even in the large House of Commons, the two five-party, or "pizza," parliaments threatened proper scrutiny despite an expanding chamber. One somewhat controversial avenue of assistance to legislators in the scrutiny function is the use of officers of Parliament. The past two decades have witnessed an almost doubling of such watchdog agencies in Canadian legislatures. While they may help overworked members, the rather scatter-gun approach to their creation suggests they are designed to solve short-term political problems and not necessarily to work with members in performing scrutiny functions.

Time and Money in Canadian Legislatures

Canadian legislatures today are, by any definition, as professional as they ever have been. Despite trends toward smaller assemblies, the resources provided to members of representative chambers have improved dramatically in the past generation. As discussed in Chapter 4,

Table 6.1

Salaries and sitting days in Canadian legislatures, 2001-2

	Base salary ($)	Average number of sitting days per annum	Cost per legislator ($)
House of Commons	131,400	129.5	1,013,289
Newfoundland and Labrador	42,796	60.0	193,773
Prince Edward Island	35,090	55.0	107,381
Nova Scotia	48,858	67.0	246,309
New Brunswick	39,550	50.0	267,272
Quebec	77,339	80.0	704,168
Ontario	82,757	52.0	868,443
Manitoba	64,250	71.0	392,284
Saskatchewan	61,800	61.0	297,224
Alberta	41,052	51.0	393,197
British Columbia	72,300	67.0	497,873
NWT	77,800	50.0	614,736
Nunavut	61,800	37.25	493,157
Yukon	34,828	60.2	174,888

Note: All provincial legislatures base their sitting days on sessions, not calendar years. However, session lengths vary widely. Cost per legislator is simply the annual budget of the assembly divided by the number of members. Nova Scotia figures are for 2000-1; all other figures for the fiscal year 2001-2.
Source: Author's survey of provincial and territorial legislative clerks, 2002.

most assemblies provide allowances for members to engage in research and hire assistants both in the capital and in the riding. Every assembly makes some staffing funding available. Yet not all assemblies are equal. Just as assemblies in the provinces differ in size, they also have different levels of professionalization. We examine three determinants of professionalization: members' compensation, the number of sitting days, and the cost per legislator of the assembly (based on Moncrief 1994).

The compensation for members differs across jurisdictions but is generally healthy (see Table 6.1). The Atlantic provinces, with fewer members and smaller assemblies, pay the least, with members in PEI and New Brunswick making under $40,000 annually (although Yukon pays least of all). Ontario MPPs are paid just over $80,000 annually. While it is still far more lucrative to be an MLA in Ontario than in PEI, the gap between incomes has decreased over time, reflecting a move toward professionalization in the less populous provinces.

The average session length varies more widely among the provinces. There is not a strong correlation between size of a legislature and how often it meets, though as Table 6.1 indicates, legislatures in the larger provinces tend to meet more often. New Brunswick, with approximately half the seats of Ontario, meets for just as long, around fifty days per year, while Manitoba sits approximately seventy days, and Quebec regularly meets over eighty days per year. The number of sitting days is generally regarded as a strong indication of professionalism. In studies of US state legislatures, those that seldom meet are often classified as "dead-end" or "springboard" (Squire 1988; Moncrief 1994). These jurisdictions either have a distrust of government and legislatively or constitutionally limit the number of times the assembly can meet (such as Texas), or they are smaller states with limited governments (such as Maine and North Dakota).

In Canada, sitting days have recently witnessed a marked change. During the 1970s and 1980s, the number of sitting days per year increased. This distribution changed somewhat beginning in the early 1990s, when even the more professional legislatures displayed a tendency to meet less. Much like the reduction in the number of seats in assemblies, the decrease has been presented to the public as limiting the government's ability to interfere in citizens' lives. Governments that meet less, spend less, is the argument. Critics offer a more skeptical explanation directly related to the scrutiny function: having fewer sitting days effectively limits the role of MLAs while further centralizing authority within the cabinet. There is some truth to this. Prime ministers and premiers have an easier time governing when they can escape facing opposition questions.

There is a wide range between jurisdictions on the cost per legislator, from a low of $107,381 in Prince Edward Island to just over a million dollars per MP in Ottawa. Yet there is a strong correlation between the size of the legislature (number of members) and cost per legislator. It is a positive, near linear relationship. Larger assemblies serve more people and cost more to operate. The exceptions are the two large territories, Nunavut and the Northwest Territories.

Legislative studies in other jurisdictions have drawn a strong correlation between the level of resources provided to an assembly and the
amount of turnover in that assembly. Findings in the United States, for
example, suggest that more professional assemblies serve to promote
political careerism (Moncrief 1994). Members of these bodies can use the
resources of the assembly not only to govern but to run for re-election.
However, in Canada there is little correlation between legislative professionalism and turnover. In fact, some of the most professional
assemblies in Canada, namely the House of Commons, Ontario, and
British Columbia, have experienced the highest levels of turnover.
Prince Edward Island, the least professional assembly, had among the
lowest levels of turnover in the 1990s. Of course jurisdictions with continued periods of one-party rule, like Alberta, tend to have lower levels
of turnover, with the majority of new members filling seats vacated by
retiring, not defeated, incumbents. The point here is that although
Canadian legislatures are becoming more professional, they have not
done so at the cost of democratic renewal.

The Problem of Size

Compared to the United States, Canadian legislatures may not seem to
fare too badly. Assemblies in the United States tend to be larger, less
driven by party leadership, and part-time. The percentage of professional, full-time legislatures south of the border is far lower than in
Canada. This division is not simply a function of state/provincial size.
Certainly states with smaller populations tend to have less professional assemblies. But larger states may also have smaller assemblies.
In the case of Texas, the constitution limits the ability of the legislature to meet more than once every two years unless called by the governor. Here the assumption is that a government that meets less governs
less. But the lack of legislative meeting time limits the ability of the
legislature to act as a check or balance to the authority of the state's
executive branch.

In Canada, the relationship between provincial size and professionalism, enunciated above, is not linear. In general larger provinces have larger assemblies. Yet the question with assemblies is not just their size, but how the members are distributed within the chamber. While Canadian legislatures might, in general, hold a healthy cohort of members, a critical mass of these members sit in the executive. These individuals do not participate in the scrutiny function; indeed, they actively avoid being caught in its trap. Removing these individuals from the cohort of legislators gives a more realistic sense of the actual number of legislators involved in the scrutiny function.

A direct comparison of the number of private members to the average cabinet size provides an important point of analysis, namely the number of members available to hold the cabinet to account (see Table 6.2). Presumably, a large assembly with a small cabinet has more "watchdogs" than a small assembly with a relatively larger cabinet. Here the differences are pronounced and telling. While Prince Edward Island may be governed effectively by an executive of twelve members, the number of men and women holding them to account in 2000 was hardly larger. Remove the speaker, and there were only fourteen private members. In terms of scrutiny, the importance of size becomes immediately more apparent. Even with over thirty cabinet ministers, the House of Commons enjoys a surfeit of members to hold the government to account. Quebec and Ontario also have a healthy number of watchdogs, though the Ontario numbers are declining. The problems are more pronounced in the less populous jurisdictions.

While smaller provinces tend to have smaller governments to complement their smaller assemblies, they deal with the same policy issues larger provinces do. The constitutionally mandated provincial jurisdiction over large policy fields like health and education is uniform across the nation. Health care is just as important to the people of Newfoundland and Labrador as it is to citizens of Ontario. Yet the backbenchers in Newfoundland are severely handicapped by their number in holding the minister to account.

More alarming is the trend toward even weaker ratios of backbenchers to cabinet ministers. A larger House of Commons and a

Table 6.2

Legislature and cabinet sizes, 1990 and 2000

Jurisdiction	Assembly size		Cabinet size		Number of private members per cabinet member	
	1990	2000	1990	2000	1990	2000
House of Commons	295	301	39	37	6.06	7.14
Newfoundland and Labrador	52	48	15	18	2.45	1.66
Prince Edward Island	32	27	11	12	1.90	1.25
Nova Scotia	52	52	22	12	1.40	3.33
New Brunswick	58	55	24	15	1.41	2.66
Quebec	125	125	30	31	3.17	3.06
Ontario	130	103	27	24	3.81	3.29
Manitoba	57	57	18	16	2.17	2.56
Saskatchewan	64	58	20	18	2.22	2.22
Alberta	83	83	25	24	2.32	2.45
British Columbia	69	79	23	28	2.00	1.82
Northwest Territories	—	19	—	7	—	1.17
Nunavut	—	19	—	8	—	1.38
Yukon	16	18	6	7	1.67	1.57

Note: Nunavut was not a territory in 1990, and data for Northwest Territories and Nunavut are therefore not provided.
Sources: Parliamentary guides; legislative websites.

significant decrease in cabinet size in Nova Scotia during the 1990s contributed to a better ratio in these two jurisdictions. Slightly smaller cabinets in Alberta and Manitoba have made only marginal differences in the cabinet-to-private-member ratio. But a smaller cabinet in Ontario has been more than offset by a large seat reduction. In British Columbia the size of the chamber was expanded, but so too was the cabinet. The net result was a decrease in the number of men and women holding the cabinet accountable.

The problem is exacerbated by single-party majorities. Not all mechanisms of scrutiny apply to government backbenchers. Questions asked by government private members during question period are not seen as challenging the government, but instead are viewed as helping the government get its message out. During debate on the speech from the throne and the budget, government private members are expected to support the executive. Few stray from this path.

Table 6.3

Opposition sizes, 2002

Jurisdiction	Assembly size	Cabinet size	Government private members	Opposition private members
House of Commons	301	37	135	129
Newfoundland and Labrador	48	18	11	19
Prince Edward Island	27	11	15	1
Nova Scotia	52	12	19	21
New Brunswick	55	15	29	11
Quebec	125	31	41	51
Ontario	103	24	34	45
Manitoba	57	16	16	25
Saskatchewan	58	18	14	26
Alberta	83	24	50	9
British Columbia	79	28	49	2
Yukon	17	7	4	6

Note: At the time of compilation vacancies existed in Quebec and Saskatchewan. The non-party territories, Nunavut and Northwest Territories, are not included.
Source: Legislative websites.

The Canadian legislative landscape favours single-party dominance. It is well documented in other studies that the single-member plurality electoral system exaggerates the impact of elections in favour of the winning party (Courtney 2004). The result is a smaller cohort of opposition members. The election results in New Brunswick in 1987 are perhaps the greatest example of this distortion, when 61 percent of the province's electorate gave the Liberal Party 100 percent of the seats. There was literally no opposition inside the legislature. While this is an extreme case, most provincial elections result in a proportion of opposition seats that is much smaller than their vote share. The problems of equality of vote are best debated elsewhere; for the purposes of scrutiny, the clear result is to put opposition members at a further disadvantage. Table 6.3 outlines the cohort of legislators not only available but publicly keen to keep the government on its toes in each jurisdiction.

The numbers alone suggest that members of the opposition in Canada face a daunting task in trying to keep up with government activity. In five jurisdictions the opposition had fewer than one dozen members in 2002, and was actually smaller than the executive. In three of these cases, moreover, the opposition was split between more than one party. In Newfoundland and Labrador the opposition had one more member than the executive, but the caucus of the official Opposition had one fewer member than the Liberal cabinet. In six jurisdictions, therefore, some members of the official Opposition had to hold down more than one critic portfolio.

In the national elected chamber, there was a strong cadre of both government and opposition private members. The cabinet enjoyed no numerical advantage. The same was true to a lesser extent in Quebec and Ontario. However, in just about every other assembly, the party distribution alone does not reveal the extent of the strain on some members. As we turn our examination to some of the basic opportunities for scrutiny, namely question period and the committee system, it becomes clearer that private members face a continual struggle in trying to keep governments accountable for their actions.

The Capacity to Ask Questions

The previous chapter outlined the nuts and bolts of question period. Theoretically, it is the greatest opportunity both for scrutiny and for participation by members of legislatures. Opposition members have cabinet ministers exactly where they want them. Ministers do not know what question is going to be asked, nor do they even know if they will be queried on any given day. When ministers do respond to a question, it is recorded in Hansard and often captured on video; a minister who gives out inaccurate information or later contradicts his or her words can be held to account for it. Further, question period can make a majority government appear weak and vulnerable. Question period should be the great equalizer, and all members should have the chance to participate in this uniquely Westminster-style proceeding.

Unfortunately the problem of numbers can severely limit the participation of legislators in the question period exercise. As discussed in Chapter 5, most question periods in Canada are dominated by leaders.

Allowing government backbenchers to throw in regular scripted questions further dilutes the true scrutiny function. One dubious upside of smaller assemblies is that fewer opposition members have to fight for the right to question the government. In addition, they have more ministers to choose from, as many members double up on critic portfolios. The problem, however, is that these critics are already overworked and stretched thin. Opposition critics are at a disadvantage tackling government ministers, who have larger staffs and the resources of an entire department at their disposal.

While the amount of chamber time dedicated to question periods across the country is generally healthy, the combination of fewer sitting days, lopsided majorities, and "lob" questions from government backbenchers does compromise the usefulness of this time as a mechanism of government accountability. Government questions, instead of being used to hold government to account, actually provide the government with a respite from heated opposition questions. On major issues, opposition parties have been able to focus their energies on a single minister. Questions from government private members provide the targeted minister with a brief opportunity to breathe more easily. In instances of minor or no opposition, questions from the government backbench take on increased significance, yet still do not serve the scrutiny function. The ability of government backbenchers to participate in this forum is not questioned here. However, it has some implications.

First, government backbenchers are less likely to ask unrehearsed questions. Cabinet ministers are therefore more likely to have a prepared answer. Further, given the unwillingness of government members to embarrass their own cabinet, their questions are far more likely to be an exercise in communication than in accountability. Although communication is a legitimate function of the government and legislature, we question its appropriateness during question period. Second, in instances of multiparty opposition, questions from government backbenchers come at the direct expense of members of the opposition. In jurisdictions with small opposition caucuses (Alberta, British Columbia, and Prince Edward Island at present), this might not be an undue restriction on the responsibilities of non-government MLAs. However, in other jurisdictions, this can create a deficit of accountability.

Stretched Thin on Committees

If scant and thinly spread opposition numbers threaten proper participation in question period, the problem faced by committees is even greater. Committees lie at the heart of a legislature's ability to probe deeply and seriously into government activity at all levels, including yearly spending within departments (via the estimates process), legislative intentions (via the committee stage of bills), and future budgetary plans (via public accounts and prebudget hearings).

Committees are run by legislators for legislators, at least in theory. They are seen to be independent of the government. In most provinces, as is the case federally, committee members select their own chair and vice-chair. In reality, the decision might be made before the first meeting of the committee and with the acquiescence of the majority government. Party leaders reserve the right to remove members of their caucus from committees, and use this lever to determine who will chair or assist the chair in a committee. However, a party can remove only a member of its own caucus. If, for example, the government wishes to punish a member by removing him or her as a committee chair, the only way to do this is to remove that member from the committee altogether. This provides some minimal protection for committee chairs and forces the government to openly express its displeasure at those who may be taking a committee in a direction not to the government's liking. Further, it provides a degree of independence to the Public Accounts Committee, which is chaired by a member of the Opposition.

As Table 6.4 indicates, legislatures in Canada have anywhere between four and twenty committees. The size of these committees ranges from a low of four MLAs in Prince Edward Island and the territories to twenty-one in the Alberta assembly. Between 1995 and 2000,

Table 6.4

Standing committee membership

| | 1995 | | 2001 | |
Jurisdiction	Number of committees	Committee size	Number of committees	Committee size
House of Commons	24	12-15	20	16-19
Newfoundland and Labrador	8	5-7	7	5-7
Prince Edward Island	8	6-8	8	4-6
Nova Scotia	9	9	9	9
New Brunswick	9	16	7	9-14
Quebec	8	10+	10	9-18
Ontario	11	12	8	8-10
Manitoba	11	11	11	11
Saskatchewan	12	12	13	7-10
Alberta	8	9-21	6	9-21
British Columbia	13	12	10	8-11
NWT	—	—	4	5-11
Nunavut	—	—	5	5
Yukon	4	5-7	4	4-7

Note: Committees include standing or legislative committees only and do not include special or occasional committees. Nunavut and NWT committees not listed for 1995 as comparison is not applicable prior to the creation of Nunavut.
Source: Author's survey of provincial and territorial legislative clerks, 2002.

most jurisdictions decreased both the number of committees and the number of members on each committee. Part of the decrease is directly associated with electoral realities. In Ontario, for example, the 1997 reduction in the number of seats was exaggerated when the third-place New Democratic Party returned only nine members, three fewer than needed for official party status. While an accommodation was reached to make nine the new floor for official party status (and the consequent right to ask questions and vote in committees), the lower overall opposition numbers meant that committee size had to be reduced.

Although committees do not all meet simultaneously, the workload for members of assemblies is very high. Beyond constituency concerns, meetings with citizens and groups, and critic roles inside the chamber and outside, committee work takes up a significant portion of a member's workday when in the capital. Members shuttle back and forth between committee meetings, House duty, and meetings in their office with constituents, interest groups, and other deputations. If anything is going to be compromised by time constraints it is most likely to be committee work, one of the most important areas.

This is due in no small part to a lack of confidence on the part of many provincial and federal lawmakers about the efficacy of committee work. While this view is held by many legislators, the problems at the national level are perhaps of greatest public concern. When important committee reports are shelved and ignored by ministers, legislators are dissuaded from putting further effort into committee work (Docherty 1999; also Gauthier 1993). As a result, unless there is a personal interest in the subject matter, or the opportunity to garner publicity, members of legislatures often treat committee work as one of their less important duties. This is not to say that members dislike the work of committees, but that in its present format, their work is not being taken seriously by governments. Chapter 7 examines more closely the important role that can and should be played by committees. For our immediate purposes the focus is on the ability of opposition members to adequately staff them.

The combination of small caucus size and large committee size means that the activities of many committees are given only cursory examination by their own members. This is particularly troubling when legislation is going through the committee stage. Although the problem is pronounced in both small and large legislatures, in small assemblies it is a regular concern. As of 2002, an exaggerated example was Prince Edward Island, where one opposition MLA had to monitor the activities of seven committees. But even in Nova Scotia, the twenty-one-person opposition was split almost evenly between the NDP and Liberals, and each party participated in six committees.

Even the larger assemblies are not immune. In Ontario, the nine-person NDP caucus in 2002 had one member in each of the eight committees. In such a case, if that member cannot attend and a substitute is not available, the party's voice is not heard. When a substitute is available, the party might register a vote or voice of opposition, but it is usually a less informed voice because the substitute is not fully abreast of the issues and cannot provide insightful comment and critique. In British Columbia, the two-person opposition was quite simply outnumbered, and could not perform any meaningful watchdog role in committees. In Alberta, there were seven committees and nine opposition MLAs.

. Saskatchewan stands out as a seeming exception. With twenty-six opposition members to sit on thirteen committees, the Saskatchewan legislature was virtually awash in watchdogs. Because these members were all in the Saskatchewan Party, they enjoyed the further luxury of being able to double up and be more than a lone voice in their respective committees. Newfoundland and Labrador also had a healthy opposition, outnumbering the government backbenchers, which could provide a more sustained accountability role in committees.

Federally, the situation of numbers was not drastic for the Alliance and Bloc, but is more disconcerting for the smaller caucuses. Though not all of the twenty House of Commons committees meet regularly, the fact that the number of committees is larger than two of the five party caucuses suggests that the watchdog function is observed in theory but not in practice on most occasions.

Assistance in the Scrutiny Function: Officers of Parliament

Members face several challenges when trying to participate in the representation and scrutiny functions. Members have access to far fewer human and financial resources than does the executive, who have the machinery of government at their disposal. The standing orders of assemblies lay out the rules that govern participation in the legislature and committees. Many rules favour full participation of individual members. Many others favour parties and the government of the day.

For members of the government backbench and those on the other side of the speaker's dais, the daunting task of government scrutiny and accountability is made somewhat easier by the work of agencies that report to the legislature and not to a minister of the Crown. At the same time, critics of these offices suggest with some credibility that the offices themselves can detract from the role of Parliament. These agents and their offices are often referred to as "officers of Parliament," though this vague term does not explain either the nature or scope of the duties of these agencies. (The speaker of a legislature may be called an officer of Parliament, but performs a far different role from the officers discussed here.) All agencies or offices of Parliament are created by acts of the legislature, and therefore their power is statutory. They carry out their mandate as delineated in the act that created them. In addition, each of these offices submits its reports (typically annually) to the speaker and not to a cabinet minister. In this sense they report to Parliament and are thus agencies of Parliament.

The agencies (or officers) that are most well known are the auditor general and the chief election officer. The auditor general examines the government books and provides yearly audits of various government departments and agencies. The chief election officer oversees the independence of the electoral system. Federally, these offices have been around since shortly after Confederation (Dobell 2002, 4). They also exist in every province.

While these are the two oldest and most familiar agencies of Parliament, there are many others. The creation of these offices can generally best be described as ad hoc (Thomas 2003). Most agencies of Parliament were established post-1960, in what might be called the modern era of Parliament. Because many of these offices were created within a short time frame and in response to external pressures, they often have little in common with one another. Most of these offices were established in one jurisdiction and then eventually created by the other legislatures. For example, the Office of Freedom of Information and the Protection of Privacy was created in Ontario in 1988; within four years it existed in four other provinces, and within ten years in two others and one territory. Our understanding of their role and function may be somewhat clouded, but so is parliamentarians'.

While different jurisdictions have different officers of Parliament, most legislatures have an auditor, chief electoral officer, information commissioner, privacy commissioner, ombudsman, and integrity commissioner. Federally, the Human Rights Commission and the commissioner of official languages are also considered officers of Parliament (Dobell 2002). The Parliament of Canada does not have an ombudsman, and as of 2002, the federal ethics counsellor reported to the prime minister and not Parliament.

The strength of these offices lies in their reporting structure. The fact that they report to Parliament (either directly to the speaker or to a standing committee) provides an important level of independence from the government. Other mechanisms, including a fixed term of office, can also provide additional independence from government (John Reid in Dobell 2002, 21). In addition, the act of reporting usually entails an opportunity for a standing committee to hear from and question the officer. This provides an additional layer of legislative scrutiny.

By far the most famous (or perhaps infamous) of these agencies is the auditor general and his or her provincial counterparts. The yearly report of the auditor is generally a source of embarrassment to the government and greeted with delight by the opposition and media. Usually chock-full of tales of highways to nowhere or programs that do little but boost the profits of advertising firms, these annual reports seldom fail to generate front-page news. Most provinces follow the federal lead on their auditor's report, and send it for more detailed examination by the Public Accounts Committee, a standing committee of the legislature chaired by an opposition member. Members of this committee are thus provided a further opportunity to keep the spotlight on ministers and departments, as they probe the findings of the auditor's report (Docherty 1999, 43).

The agencies/officers of Parliament can provide an additional type of scrutiny of the government. Yet there are limits to the role that can be played by officers of Parliament. In addition, it is not clear that these agencies enjoy the support of parliamentarians. While they report to Parliament, they do not serve Parliament, and therefore are seldom in a position to work with Parliament. The auditor general is a case in point. Beyond embarrassing the government, there is little evidence that the auditor general either works in consort with members of the Commons, or even enjoys a strong reporting relationship with them. The Public Accounts Committee has no power to direct the auditor general's office to investigate any department or government agency (Gauthier 1993). As a result, members cannot use the resources of this office for accountability or scrutiny purposes. Nor do they have the ability to scrutinize the workings of this office (Docherty 1999, 45). Finally, academics have suggested that successive auditor generals have stepped over the bounds of scrutiny to engage in a form of policy making that might not enjoy the support of either the government or members of Parliament (Sutherland 1986). As a result, there is concern among academics and legislators that auditors' reports tend to be one- or two-day media events that, in the words of former public accounts chair Jean-Robert Gauthier (1993, 9), build up "populist appeal and street power at the expense of representative institutions of government and Parliament."

The relationship among legislatures, agencies that report to them, and legislators has yet to fully develop. Part of the strain in the development of this relationship is due to the rather ill-defined nature of these offices. Some, such as the auditor, election officer, and provincial ombudsman, have been around for decades, and an institutional memory and long-standing relationships have developed. The associations may be strained at times, and there may be competing visions, but roles of all the players are at least defined.

The growth of new offices in the past two decades has forced new understandings of scrutiny of government and new relationships between parliaments and parliamentary officers in Canada. It has also called into question the role of Parliament in the scrutiny and accountability function. Some officers are necessary and their independent roles are vital. But the fact that different jurisdictions have different agencies has led to speculation that some agencies might be political creations. Ontario, for example, has an environment commissioner who reports to the speaker, as mandated by the government's 1994 Environmental Bill of Rights. The environment commissioner can appear before a standing committee of the legislature, and provides a platform for environmental concerns. Although it is difficult to argue against having an environment commissioner charged with protecting the air and water that citizens breathe and drink, it is at heart a political decision to give preference to this office over, say, the Ontario Human Rights Commission, which reports to the legislature indirectly through the Ministry of Citizenship. In Saskatchewan, the children's advocate officer is an officer of the assembly. The Ontario counterpart, the Children's Secretariat, falls under the jurisdiction of Children and Youth Services and thus reports to a minister and not to all legislators.

Perhaps the most political decision regarding officers of Parliament has been the ongoing debate over the federal ethics counsellor. Created as part of the 1993 Liberal Red Book campaign platform, the office was originally intended to be an office of Parliament and thus report to Parliament. The decision of Prime Minister Chrétien to have the ethics counsellor report to him instead has justified critics in questioning the independence of the office and thus the integrity of its reports. In March 2004 the federal government finally fulfilled a long held promise to create an ethics commissioner who would report to the House of Commons. The Speaker will receive the first annual report no later than June 2005. Nine of ten provinces and all three territories have an ethics commissioner or conflict of interest officer who reports directly to the legislature.

As long as political controversy surrounds the creation and function of these offices, the extent of their contribution to the scrutiny exercise will always be debatable. In addition, the increasing willingness of governments to turn to officers and agencies of Parliament can be seen as a threat to the ability of members to properly perform their function. Proponents of these bodies might well be correct in claiming that if a legislature were properly undertaking the scrutiny task, additional agencies would be unnecessary. The statutory objectives of these bodies do not directly conflict with the role of members: they all serve an accountability or scrutiny function. However, the increased number of these agencies, and the rather ad hoc approach that successive governments across the country have taken in their creation, suggest that the organizations often reflect governmental and not legislative policy objectives. If this is the case, legislators might increasingly find themselves scrutinizing the agencies that were established for the same purpose.

Conclusion

Arguing for more politicians is akin to arguing for higher taxes or unpleasant medical tests. Even if people agree, they are not likely to support this position publicly. Yet the problem of size is real for many legislatures in Canada, including the House of Commons. Of course, the problem is not size alone, but rather the combination of size, cabinet government, and an electoral system that minimizes the seats of opposition parties far below the level their electoral support actually warrants.

Legislatures act as watchdogs on the government. In order to perform this function properly, they need two things: adequate resources and a critical mass of members. In Canada, most legislatures are moving in the right direction in terms of resources. It is possible to be a full-time member of an opposition party nationally, provincially, and territorially in Canada. Given that these individuals are watching full-time politicians, usually with a large staff and the resources of an entire government department at their disposal, this is a minimum criterion. Additional staffing and constituency offices are available to all MPs and most MLAs. These resources go a long way to allowing members to concentrate on their watchdog function while in the capital.

In terms of the latter requirement, a critical mass, legislatures in Canada fare less well. Small opposition parties are stretched to, first, research, and second, participate actively in all the accountability mechanisms available to them. Question period is off-limits for parties that do not enjoy official recognition, and the amount of time provided to government backbenchers comes at the expense of opposition parties. Poor rules that do not require regular attendance of cabinet ministers only exacerbate this problem. The ability of members, particularly opposition members, to effectively function in committees is also open to question. Small caucuses face great difficulty in staying on top of issues, properly preparing for meetings, and critically examining proposed legislation when they are constantly rushing from one committee to another, or covering for a colleague on a committee that falls outside the critic roles (of which there is often more than one).

Perhaps the biggest concern, however, is the trend in many jurisdictions. Assemblies in Canada are small and getting smaller. Despite larger populations, increased concerns over public policies, and steady cabinet sizes, the actual assemblies are shrinking. This means fewer people doing more work.

In terms of democratic representation, the problem is one of accountability. While it makes political hay to reduce the size of legislatures on the theory that fewer politicians means less spending, this is hardly a truism. In fact, available evidence suggests the contrary. In Ontario in 1997 the cost per provincial legislator was just over $684,000, for a total legislative budget of over $70 million for 130 MPPs. In 2002 the streamlined chamber of 103 MPPs had a cost per legislator of over $868,000 for a total legislative budget of just under $90 million. Smaller is not cheaper. In the end all it really means is fewer people charged with keeping the government honest and on its toes. We have not reduced the size of government but the size of its watchdog. Government rolls merrily along.

CHAPTER 6

Strengths

- Although four- and five-party parliaments have resulted in more, but generally smaller, caucuses at the federal level, the official Opposition and third party have consistently elected enough MPs to perform their scrutiny functions properly and to participate fully.

- Officers of parliament aid in the scrutiny function by acting as a further watchdog on the government. Legislatures have nonetheless yet to agree on the scope and role of such officers. Critics argue that they can be used to help the executive avoid responsibility rather than be held accountable.

Weaknesses

- There has been a trend at the provincial level to decrease the size of legislative assemblies. This decrease does not always include decreasing the size of cabinet.

- In smaller assemblies, the number of officials who raise and spend public monies has stayed relatively constant while the number of individuals charged with keeping them accountable has decreased.

- Because of smaller caucus sizes, members in provincial assemblies have been stretched too thin on committees and do not have the proper resources to be fully effective.

- Exacerbating the problem of size, provincial assemblies are sitting for fewer days per year, thus avoiding the executive's responsibility to be accountable for their activities.

THE LEGISLATIVE PROCESS

7

One of the most important functions of a Westminster legislature is to debate and pass or defeat legislation that the government has introduced. In times of majority governments this process too often appears a mere formality, but it is essential for the development of good public policy. Even though governments usually get their way, the requirement that bills pass through the legislative process is critical to good democratic practice. Beyond the symbolic (but nonetheless important) understanding that legislatures provide legitimacy for laws, the legislative process has practical benefits. Governments can use committees to hear from citizens, fine-tune legislation, and amend their own legislation. Governments recognize that all members can play important, though at times disruptive, roles in the legislative process.

The trick for governments is to try to find a balance that maintains their own agenda while allowing for proper participation of all members. This is the road map to successful legislative governance (Atkinson and Docherty 2000). It is not easily accomplished. Particularly in multiparty parliaments, government and opposition seldom share objectives. When opposition parties try to slow down a government's legislative plans, the government is tempted to close ranks and allow less time for debate and discussion on pending legislation. When the government provides opposition parties too much latitude, it can appear weak and run the risk of not fulfilling its election promises. This chapter examines how legislatures and governments try to maintain some form of balance in the legislative process, focusing on government legislation and the committee system.

Legislative Agenda of Governments

The government (i.e., the executive) has the opportunity to present formally its legislative and policy agenda to the legislature on two occasions: the speech from the throne and the budget. These occasions allow the government to spell out both how it intends to fulfill its electoral mandate and to manage its fiscal responsibilities in spending public monies. The government can also respond to situations that have developed since its election.

SPEECH FROM THE THRONE

The throne speech formally opens the beginning of each legislative session. The title indicates the event's history and meaning. Historically, British parliaments were opened by the monarch, who called Parliament to request funds. The king or queen addressed members of Parliament when they first met, and explained why the funds were needed. Immediately afterward, the government would introduce a piece of legislation that had not been in the throne speech, in order to establish legislative and governmental independence from the Crown. In Canadian assemblies the throne speech is read by the Queen's representatives, federally by the governor general and provincially by lieutenant governors. In Quebec, the throne speech has been replaced by an inaugural address by the premier, though the lieutenant governor attends the event. This change, introduced in 1969, was one of several moves undertaken by successive Quebec governments to decrease the profile of the monarchy in legislative and governmental life (Massicotte 1989, 72-5).

We might be tempted to think of the speech from the throne as an historical relic that serves little purpose beyond allowing a government to repeat its election promises and maintaining a ceremonial role for the head of state. Nonetheless, the throne speech and the legislation that flows from it are central to successful governing and act as inducements to reinforce party discipline on all sides of the House. This is achieved in two ways.

First, following the actual speech from the throne, six days are set aside for legislative debate on the speech. Acceptance of the speech is moved and seconded by government backbenchers, once again to indicate independence from the Crown. More practically, the six days of debate allow new members an opportunity to participate inside the chamber. Members use this opportunity to talk about the concerns of their constituents and how the government's plans either address or ignore the challenges facing their individual ridings. Although routinely ignored by the media and other legislative observers, this is an important opportunity for participation for rookie MPs. At the same time, the speeches by new (and veteran) members quickly stake out the positions of the parties.

Second, since much of the throne speech at the opening of a new Parliament comes from election platforms, almost all bills that flow from the speech are considered matters of confidence for the government. That is, should a government lose a vote on legislation that was discussed in the throne speech, its ability to continue to govern would be seriously jeopardized. As a result, the governing party whip is cracked very harshly on these matters. Most opposition whips are equally stringent, if only to ensure that their MPs are consistent with their own party platform.

Most governments have two (occasionally three) speeches from the throne. The initial speech when Parliament first meets after a general election is likely to repeat campaign pledges. The second occurs at approximately the halfway point of a government's life, when the prime minister (or premier) asks the governor general (or lieutenant governor) to conclude the parliamentary session, or prorogue Parliament without dissolving it. Doing the latter would force an election.

Here the government wants to end the legislative session and start fresh.

When a Parliament has prorogued, all government bills not yet passed "die" on the order paper. Any bill introduced but not passed must be reintroduced afresh in the next session. The ability of governments to choose when to end a legislative session is a powerful tool. A bill that received a rough ride in committee, or a bill that the government felt compelled to introduce but was not ready to see become law, can be most effectively postponed by ending a parliamentary session. This is not an uncommon occurrence, though it is more likely with controversial legislation that the government is uncomfortable moving forward at that particular time.

In addition, prorogation allows a government to have a new speech from the throne when Parliament reconvenes. This permits the government to turn its attention to matters that have arisen since the election, or to forge ahead in a different direction. In the latter instance legislative proposals that might not have been part of an election manifesto, or perhaps even agreed to in caucus, very quickly have the weight of confidence attached to them. Members of the governing party are placed in an awkward position, because they are asked to treat new matters – some of which never passed caucus – as the equivalent of election promises.

Perhaps the most controversial recent example was the speech from the throne opening the second session of the thirty-seventh Parliament in September 2002. Much of the throne speech listed proposals that were widely regarded as part of Prime Minister Chrétien's so-called legacy (McCarthy 2002b). Some of the issues raised derived from previous election platforms, but others were new. One seemingly innocuous sentence in the speech committed the government to "introducing legislative changes to the financing of political parties and candidates for office" (Commons 2002a, 1). Once the details of this plan were revealed, many Liberal MPs were surprised to find that the prime minister was proposing to reduce dramatically the ability of parliamentarians, challengers, and political parties to raise money. Not only did this strike some as hypocritical – the retiring prime minister was establishing laws he would not have to live under – but they were then told that this was a matter of confidence in their own government (Taber 2002; also Docherty 2004; Atkinson and Docherty 2004).

While there was a great deal of humour in the prime minister's threat to call a snap election if his backbench did not go along with this legislation (it is hard to imagine a retiring leader calling for a mandate from Canadians to rein in the caucus for his or her remaining months in office), it did point to the real problem that confidence can create. Backbenchers who have little input into their own government's legislative agenda are asked to blindly support legislation they may not have even seen. A speech from the throne that reiterates an election platform does not compromise elected government members. However, one that opens a second session and contains vague general promises that are transformed into larger legislative packages can effectively handcuff the very members of Parliament the government looks to for support.

Budget

The second formal occasion for the government to present a legislative and economic agenda to the legislature is the introduction of the budget. The budget and the bills that flow from it are all part of the minister of finance's economic platform that directly spells out the state of the nation's finances and the fiscal plan of the government for the next year. What follows is a brief description of the federal budget and its legislative implications. The budgetary processes in the provinces are similar.

The bulk of the decisions surrounding the budget (both spending and revenue plans) are made by a combination of cabinet committees and officials in the Department of Finance. The federal budget is usually tabled in February, though elections or other political events have been known to change the scheduling. The budget is tabled before the tabling of the estimates (the line-by-line spending of departments).

The budgetary process allows all members of Parliament many access points for oral participation. First is the actual budget speech itself. The minister of finance places a motion in the legislature that the Parliament supports the budgetary policies of the government. This is effectively a vote of endorsement for the budget. With the budget speech that follows, the motion kicks off four days of debate on the budget. Much like the debate following the speech from the throne, the budget debate is a general debate focusing on the economic, fiscal, and social plans of the government. It is also seen as a matter of confidence in the government. Traditionally, any government that loses the motion must tell the governor general that it no longer enjoys the confidence of the House. Not surprisingly, budget debates have a very tight whip from all parties, and majority governments in Canada never lose a budget motion. The last time a federal budget motion was defeated was during the minority Joe Clark government of 1979; the vote that brought down the government was an amendment to the original motion (Simpson 1980, 15).

Following the debate on the budget speech are debates on all of the bills needed to provide legislative authority to the government's plans. Remembering that only the Crown can introduce "money bills" – legislation causing a direct spending or raising of tax dollars – each of these bills is introduced by the minister of finance or the minister of the relevant department. Each of these bills is also considered a matter of confidence in the government. As a result, a tight whip is in place for all budget bills, which are treated the same as the budget speech and throne speech.

One complication in the budget process arises from the fact that most tax increases on items are implemented immediately, on the day after the introduction of the budget. As well as encouraging Canadians to stock up on alcohol, cigarettes, and other so-called sin items (often the first to be hit with tax increases) on budget day, tax increases are implemented without formal legislative approval. Because the implementation bills are often not passed until well after the budget debate has finished, proposed legislation for tax increases often employs retroactive dates. This limits any potential amendments that might be applied to a budget bill.

A now inaccessible page on the Parliament website explained the situation well: a budget proposal to increase the taxes on gasoline by three cents a litre might take effect at midnight after the budget is read. The implementation bill might not pass for some time, but would permit the taxes to be raised retroactively. One can scarcely imagine the administrative nightmare if the bill were amended to an increase of only two cents per litre. Canadians might feel entitled to a one-cent reimbursement for every litre of gas purchased during this period! Retroactivity thus heightens party discipline and reduces the function of members of Parliament in the passing of budget legislation to an almost pro forma role.

Traditionally, the contents of budgets were tightly held secrets, and any leaked budget information would result in calls for the minister of finance to resign. The logic behind such secrecy was that any leaked information might provide a particular sector of the economy or a particular firm with an undue advantage. This convention was taken so seriously that the most dedicated investigative reporters were known to scour through shredded Department of Finance papers hoping for pre-budget leaks. Among finance ministers who faced pressure to resign after indirect leaks in his department was Conservative Michael Wilson during the Mulroney era (Howard 1989). Confidentiality surrounding budget contents allowed finance ministers to limit legislative participation in the creation of the budget. Party discipline then eliminated meaningful participation after the budget has been introduced. Without any input before the budget, members of Parliament were effectively prevented from engaging in the major fiscal policies of the state.

But no reasonable justification exists for not holding open prebudget consultations. Prebudget deliberations have always existed in the Department of Finance. Ministers of finance and officials in the department receive regular advice (some solicited, some not) from business and economic interests and organizations (Lindquist 1985, 18-20). Budgets have never been written in a vacuum, though advice was generally from the financial and not social sector (Archer et al. 2002, 257).

There had long been a call for greater public participation in the prebudget consultation process. As far back as 1984, the Royal Commission on the Economic Union and Development Prospects for Canada recommended that a committee of the House of Commons be charged with hearing from the public and submitting a prebudget report to the minister of finance. Neither the Trudeau government that had established the commission nor the Mulroney government that succeeded the Liberals saw fit to introduce this reform. Provincially, the Ontario government introduced the practice during the Liberal-NDP accord period, 1985-7 (White 1989, 159).

Federally, it was not until 1994, as part of many changes to the standing orders, that the Standing Committee on Finance was charged with making recommendations on the government's budgetary proposals. This allowed the committee to hear from the public before the drafting of the budget. The committee now holds hearings in the late fall and reports to the minister of finance in December. This small move made the prebudget consultation process far more transparent, allowed open participation by the interested public, and opened the door to participation in monetary policy by private members. Given the tight party discipline on budget legislation, it is far easier to have an open discussion on budget policy before it is read in the Commons. Prebudget hearings by a committee of the legislature have thus dramatically improved participation in the legislative process.

The move toward opening up the budgetary process did not end with prebudget hearings, which may themselves have encouraged other changes. One of the biggest reforms, undertaken by Finance Minister Paul Martin in 1994, was to lift the veil from budget secrecy. The minister of finance took the unusual step of revealing his general budgetary intentions and directions before the budget. Admittedly, he had some selfish reasons for this move. His first few budgets contained major spending reductions and had negative impacts on the provinces (Cameron 1995, 159-84; also Rice 1995, 185-7). By revealing directions early, the minister had time to build support for his austerity measures (Archer et al. 2002, 257). However, the long-term effect of this openness was to call into question the historical hysteria over budget secrecy. All a minister of finance had to do was openly announce his or her general intentions; as long as the plans did not have an impact on markets or specific companies there would be no conflict. The removal of budget secrecy also allows a greater sense of participation among citizens and groups seeking to proffer their advice (Lindquist 1985, 25). Openness was thus a prerequisite to more meaningful consultation in the budgetary process.

Government Legislation

While every bill in a parliamentary system has three readings, the term is a misnomer. While one hopes that those voting on a bill will indeed read it at some point in time, this is not done during the reading stage. The term "reading" refers to the process in which the title of each piece of legislation is read before it is put to a vote in the legislature. Each of the three readings denotes a stage of the bill's passage through the legislative process.

The first stage, or reading, is when the bill is introduced, though technically the introduction of the bill and the first reading occur separately. A bill is introduced when a member stands in his or her place and literally introduces the legislation, before the first vote. Practices vary in Canadian legislatures, but typically the person who introduces the bill can make a short speech in its favour. The first reading and subsequent vote are little more than a formality. Typically, the minister responsible introduces the bill. Pieces of government legislation are known as "public bills," to distinguish them from private members' bills and from "private bills," which deal with a specific corporation or municipality. Opposition parties may vote for or against the bill, but rarely comment on it. Because legislation is introduced in Parliament, it is only after first reading that a bill is available in printed form, or (more recently) on-line. In some cases, the positions of parties on bills are established well before their introduction. But without speeches from the recognized parties, no views are recorded in Hansard on the merits or drawbacks of the bill.

Second reading, or the debate on the principles of the bill, is the first substantive stage for legislation. Members debate the substance of the bill and more formally stake out their positions on the essentials of the legislation. The government controls the timing of its legislation and dictates when debates and votes will occur. In addition, most legislatures in Canada have provided governments with the ability to limit the amount of debate on a bill if necessary. In the federal House of Commons, there is no limit on the amount of debate on the second reading of bills. However, the length of speeches by members is limited. At the second reading stage, there can be no changes offered to the bill. Bills are debated in principle, so that opposition – and even government – members can only make suggestions about improving the legislation. Changes cannot be made until after second reading.

After second reading, legislation typically goes through a committee stage. Amendments can be tabled, discussed, and voted on in either a legislative or standing committee or the "committee of the whole." Legislative and standing committees are subgroups of members of the legislature comprised of all recognized parties in proportion to their respective seat totals; a legislative committee is established to examine a specific bill. A committee of the whole is any and all members of the assembly who meet as a committee inside the actual legislative chamber. When the committee of the whole meets the speaker must leave his or her chair, and a chairperson presides over the proceedings (Marleau and Montpetit 2000, 774-6). Here normal parliamentary rules are relaxed and the debate is freer than in the traditional legislative setting.

Limits on the type of amendments are identical in all types of committee, but the differences between committee of the whole and other committees can be profound. Despite the relaxation of formalities, the legislature invokes a sense of seriousness and partisanship that can be refreshingly avoided in committees. A sense of collegiality is more easily obtained away from the actual legislative chamber. As a result, the opportunity for more nonpartisan engagement is greater in a legislative or standing committee than it is in the committee of the whole. Standing or legislative committees allow greater participation in the

Table 7.1

Legislative committees: Bills and witnesses

Jurisdiction	Bill sent to committee after second reading	Bill can be referred after first reading	Committee has power to call witnesses
House of Commons	Yes	Yes, but occurs rarely	Yes
Newfoundland and Labrador	No, with rare exceptions	No, but can look at draft legislation	Yes, but typically on nonlegislative matters
Prince Edward Island	Occurs rarely (less than 10 percent)	Yes, but occurs rarely	Yes
Nova Scotia	Yes	No	Yes
New Brunswick	Occurs rarely (less than 2 percent)	No	Yes
Quebec	Yes	Yes, but occurs rarely	Yes
Ontario	Requires 8 members to refer bill if government does not send it to committee	Yes, but occurs rarely	Yes
Manitoba	Yes	No	Yes
Saskatchewan	Yes	Yes	Yes
Alberta	No, bills heard and amended in committee of the whole	No	Yes, but typically on nonlegislative matters
British Columbia	No, bills heard and amended in committee of the whole	Yes, but occurs rarely	Yes, rarely does on public bills but frequently on other matters
Northwest Territories	Yes	No	Yes
Nunavut	Yes	No	Yes
Yukon	Occurs rarely (once since 1990)	Yes, but has never occurred	Yes

Source: Author's survey of provincial and territorial legislative clerks, 2002; standing orders.

legislative process, because they can decide to hold hearings and invite comment from the public. Legislators can then hear from witnesses.

Table 7.1 illustrates how the different legislatures refer bills to committees, if at all. Many Canadian legislatures do not routinely send their public bills to standing or legislative committees after second reading. Alberta and British Columbia amend and hold clause-by-clause debate on legislation in a committee of the whole. Nova Scotia and Quebec follow the federal example of automatic referral, as do the two non-party-based territories, Nunavut and the Northwest Territories. Other legislatures have rarely used provisions for standing or select committees to study and amend government legislation. In New Brunswick and Prince Edward Island, less than 10 percent of all bills are sent to a legislative or standing committee. It is more usual for clause-by-clause debate and voting on legislation to occur in a committee of the whole.

Ontario sends a bill either to a legislative or standing committee or to committee of the whole at the discretion of the minister sponsoring the bill. However, a provision in the provincial standing orders allows eight members standing in their places to have any bill sent to a standing committee (Ontario 1999, 72[c]). This de facto allows any recognized opposition party to send a government bill to a committee. Of course once there, the bill is in the hands of the majority of committee members, which is usually to say the government. The committee may or may not then decide to hold hearings on the bill. In other words, an opposition-sponsored referral may have more symbolic than real significance.

Legislative or standing committees have one enormous freedom that committees of the whole do not enjoy, namely to hear from the public. In those jurisdictions where legislation is debated and amended in committee of the whole, members have no opportunity to hear from witnesses. It is impractical to hear from witnesses during committee of the whole House. Legislatures in Ontario, Quebec, and the Northwest Territories, like the federal House of Commons, routinely send bills to committees and these committees routinely seek public input. As the final column of Table 7.1 indicates, all legislatures provide for public participation via standing or select committees, though in many cases not during the passing of legislation. If bills are not sent to committee the public therefore has little opportunity to comment formally on the matter.

The ability of citizens and groups to publicly address legislators on legislative matters should be seen as the minimum standard for participatory governance. And many Canadians engage in this activity on a regular basis. Thousands appear in front of Commons committees each year, though the number that testify on actual bills is far fewer (McInnes 1999, 1). Further, committees can travel across the country or province much more easily than many citizens can make the trip to the capital. Sending bills to committees after second reading allows greater participation from both legislators and the public.

Jurisdictions that regularly use legislative or standing committees in the passing of legislation do not do so at the expense of the committee of the whole. Many pieces of legislation that have been fine-tuned, debated, and changed in committee have last-minute amendments made in committee of the whole *after* they are reported back to the legislature. Often these last-minute changes are minor and procedural, making the legislation compatible with other statutes. In other cases the changes reflect concerns of the committee or a better understanding of some problems with the legislation as presented. In any case the lesson is clear: some legislation requires a second look. Committees can debate, hear from witnesses, and proceed with clause-by-clause voting and amendments, all relatively shielded from the more blatant partisan nature of the floor of the assembly. The government can still make use of committee of the whole after a bill has been reported.

The importance of hearing from witnesses and of clause-by-clause, informed, but informal debate in the legislative process has led proponents of reform to call for greater use of committees. In particular, advocates of reform suggest sending significant legislation to committee directly from first reading. In the United Kingdom, following his first successful majority in 1997, Tony Blair introduced this practice among other reforms to Westminster. Bills can now be printed in draft form and then sent directly to committees for study. This occurs at the government's discretion and while not typical practice has been used effectively. Of course, the more a government is committed to a particular piece of legislation, the less freedom there is to provide it to committees for alteration (Norton 2000, 90-2). In Canada, the House of Commons has had the option of sending bills to committees after first reading since 1994, and Ontario's standing orders have permitted it since 1999. In neither case, however, does it occur regularly. In fact, in Ottawa the practice has been used less since 1998 than when it was first introduced. In Ontario it was used only seven times between 1999 and 2002, and the bills were either uncontroversial or not overtly partisan (Ontario 2002, 21-2).

The justification for more immediate referrals to committee is that the committee process allows broader debate and amendments. After second reading, partisan lines have already been drawn, and the scope of amendments is necessarily limited to the thrust of the bill as written by the government. If a bill is sent earlier, i.e., after first reading, the report of the committee is less constrained. Members of the legislature can then solicit public feedback on a matter that might not have initially been subject to a wider public debate. In this case, the report of a committee might include sweeping amendments and a change in course that reflects public support.

The final benefit of such scrutiny is that it does not diminish the power of the government to control its own agenda. The government House leader still decides when a piece of legislation will be called for debate and can choose simply to withhold voting on a bill. Committee study does not force a government to call for resolution on a bill, nor does it force a government to retract from a public position. Indeed, prelegislative study might avoid the embarrassing situations governments sometimes face when they come to clause-by-clause debate with more amendments than the opposition parties have. A government can allow public feedback without putting political capital on the line.

It is too soon to tell if sending bills to committee after first reading more frequently will produce the predicted results. Early indications are that it enhances the participation of private members without unduly constraining governments. In Great Britain, this move has been seen as expanding the role for private members beyond mere followers or adversaries of the executive (Riddell 2000, 250). In Ontario, the Standing Committee on the Legislative Committee recently called for increased use of prelegislative scrutiny. Its report argued that on those occasions when the practice had been employed, the results were beneficial to the government, to the public, and to private members (Ontario 2002).

Once a bill is reported from committee it is sent back to the legislature as amended. Federally, this is known as the report stage. If the

bill has been to a standing or legislative committee it might be subject to some final fine-tuning in committee of the whole, where other
members have the opportunity to propose amendments. Otherwise it
is ready for final debate and a vote on its third reading. The debate on
third reading is the final chance for members to state their views on
the bill officially, on the public record. After the vote on third reading
a provincial piece of legislation has only one final stage, royal assent.

Federally, a bill must also pass the Senate, and if the bill is passed
in a different form, the House must either accept the Senate's version
of the legislation or try to work out a compromise. The appointed
Senate has been very reticent to actually stop legislation, though that
authority does exist constitutionally (Archer et al. 2002, 182). In many
ways this power exists only when it is not used. The last time the
Senate threatened to use its veto occurred during the now-infamous
GST debate, when Prime Minister Mulroney turned to a little-known
constitutional provision to appoint additional senators. While the
public had little stomach for a 7 percent goods and services tax, neither were Canadians enthralled that an unelected chamber was trying
to stymie an elected government (Campbell and Pal 1991, 394-9).

Royal assent indicates that the monarch, or his or her Canadian
representative, signs the bill into law. The statute or law comes into
effect either immediately or at a later date prescribed by the government. A bill has no legal status until it is given royal assent.
Governments control the timing of royal assent and can delay this
stage if they deem it necessary.

Restrictions on Participation: Closure and Time Allocation

Despite the ability of some legislatures to either hear from witnesses
or send bills to committees, the government still holds most of the
cards in terms of moving its own agenda. Even when opposition parties try to delay legislation, the rules of assemblies still provide the

government with the upper hand. The best way for governments to ensure speedy passage of legislation is to limit the debate.

This can be done either through closure or time allocation. Of these two measures, the former is viewed as the more drastic. Closure (also called cloture), occurs when the government moves that there can be no adjournment on the debate of a bill (that is, the legislature cannot adjourn for the day and resume debate the next day); at the end of the sitting, the legislature must vote on the bill. Closure can occur at any stage of a bill (first through third readings) or on any motion (Marleau and Montpetit 2000). Closure effectively stops debate on any bill. It is rarely used by governments, as it allows the opposition to claim that the government is short-circuiting the democratic process by silencing dissenting voices. Among the most famous examples in Canadian history is the pipeline debate of 1956, when the St. Laurent government imposed closure at all three readings (Pelletier 2000, 2).

Time allocation grew out of the negative reaction to the use of closure by the federal government. As part of standing order reforms in 1971, the Trudeau government amended the rules of procedure to allow the government to set specific periods for debate on government bills. The changes allowed the government to allocate debating times with – or more controversially without – the consent of the opposition parties. As Pelletier (2000, 3) notes, this latter provision forced Trudeau to use closure to pass his reform package. Time allocation is seen as less restrictive than closure because the legislature can adjourn without voting on a bill.

While governments may be reticent to use closure or time allocation, they are faced with the need to pass their legislative agenda. If the opposition is threatening to use the standing orders to try to delay passage of a bill, the pressure increases to limit the amount of time designated for debate. If opposition parties routinely delay the debate and passage of legislation, governments become more inclined to use time allocation. The use of closure may be a signal that the legislature is not functioning properly. As discussed in Chapter 3, while the legislative calendar is controlled by the government (and the government House

Table 7.2

Use of time allocation and closure on government legislation and motions

Jurisdiction	Closure	Time allocation
House of Commons	6	37
British Columbia	1	1
Alberta	14	0
Saskatchewan	7	5
Manitoba	0	0
Ontario	11 (6 years)	76 (6 years)
Quebec	0	3-4
New Brunswick	0	0
Nova Scotia	0	0
Prince Edward Island	0	0
Newfoundland and Labrador	1	4
Yukon	Provided for in rules only as of 2001	
Northwest Territories	0	Not provided for in rules
Nunavut	0	0

Note: Provincial and territorial clerks were asked how many times the government had used time allocation in a five-year period. Variance on this point in their answers is indicated in parentheses. House of Commons information covers the calendar years 1998-2002.
Sources: Author's survey of provincial and territorial legislative clerks, 2002; Library of Parliament.

leader in particular), it is usually agreed to during weekly meetings of all the House leaders. When the various House leaders work well together, there is enough compromise that time allocation or closure is not necessary.

When governments invoke closure or time allocation they often point to the opposition as being obstreperous and blocking the will of the people. Governments enjoy the support of the House and cannot be hamstrung by an opposition that wishes to stall legislation that may have broad public support. Additionally the government can suggest that its legislative agenda is so ambitious that limiting debate is the only possible way to see it through. (That said, when governments do not resort to closure they rarely state that they have no legislative agenda to speak of, or that the opposition is being very cooperative.)

Most Canadian legislatures do not resort to closure or time allocation, but several use them often. One of the most striking things about Table 7.2 is its extremes. None of the Maritime provinces and only two western provinces use either method. Polarized legislatures seem no more likely to resort to closure than collegial assemblies are. British Columbia, despite one of the most notoriously divided legislatures, used closure and time allocation only once each between 1995 and 2001, while Alberta, with a one-party dominant system, used closure an average of almost three times per year.

Ontario's use of closure is striking. Closure was used most often during the first year of the Mike Harris government, 1995, when the Conservatives used it seven times. Time allocation was deployed twenty times during this same period. But even excluding this year, Ontario was second only to Alberta in use of closure and used time allocation more than any other provincial assembly. Whether because of a vociferous opposition or a government unwilling to listen, the Ontario legislature simply was not working well during the 1995-2001 period. The House leaders were unable to agree to a legislative timetable that allowed both the government to have its legislation and the opposition to have its debate.

The House of Commons is far more inclined to use time allocation than closure. The use of time allocation increased substantially after the 1997 general election, when there were five officially recognized parties able to participate in all legislative matters. In the thirty-fifth Parliament, with three recognized parties, time allocation was used twenty times on 152 passed pieces of legislation. In the thirty-sixth Parliament, with five recognized parties, it was imposed twenty-nine times on 95 passed pieces of legislation (Pelletier 2000, 8). Time allocation was used primarily on major bills, some of which had support from some of the opposition parties but faced strong resistance from others. Among the bills for which time allocation was used at more than one stage were the Clarity Act on Quebec secession, the Nisga'a Treaty, and legislation extending federal benefits to same-sex couples (13). The importance of debate in the legislative process may be threatened by an increased reliance on time allocation.

In some jurisdictions the use of time allocation or closure has less to do with the strength of the opposition and more to do with the government's desire to avoid the legislature. Part of the problem stems from the decrease in sitting days. As discussed more extensively in Chapter 6, when a legislature meets less often, it has less time to hear debate. If it still hopes to proceed with an ambitious agenda – such as Mike Harris's "Common Sense Revolution" – the only option is to limit debate, and therefore decrease opportunities for participation by all members. While this may make for efficient government, it does not make for a good working legislative environment.

Finally, we should recognize that on occasion limiting debate might be desirable. For example, in the case of the Nisga'a Treaty, the government had the support of some of the opposition parties in its move to pass the treaty. Government must be able to bring its legislation to a vote. If one party decides to bog down the legislature, time allocation can be used to resolve legislative stalemates. When the government has the support of some opposition parties to resort to time allocation, it can appear responsive to public demands.

Constraints on Representation: Party Discipline and Matters of Confidence

For observers of Parliament in Canada, party discipline is something akin to bad weather: everyone complains, but nobody seems able to do anything about it. The notion that members must stick to a particular party line contradicts the fundamental understanding that many Canadians have of representation, namely that members vote in accordance with the wishes of their constituents. Canadians believe that elected officials too often follow the dictates of party leaders (Clarke et al. 1996, 177-9). This belief that members are not representing constituents is at the root of the so-called democratic deficit.

The problem is that this understanding of representation is too simplistic and runs counter to the principles of parliamentary government. The first priority for a government in a Westminster model is to maintain the confidence of the legislative assembly. If it cannot do that, it cannot govern. The executive must always ensure that it enjoys the confidence of the majority of members and the consequent legitimacy to govern (Docherty 1997, 138). The government can function only know-ing that it will not be defeated (Franks 1987, 35). In times of majority governments, the simplest and most effective way to maintain confi-dence is for the government party to support the government.

While party discipline and confidence are necessary for the govern-ment, they are also desirable for parties in opposition. Indeed, there is a strong reliance on party discipline on both sides of the speaker's dais. Any opposition party that is facing major internal dissension can never hope to place a united platform in front of voters. Opposition parties can afford to have a few votes when members break ranks, but too many of these and the party risks becoming seriously fractured. Stockwell Day's problems in leading the Alliance were in part due to the party caucus's inability to remained unified (Laghi 2002a). Party discipline and solidarity are closely linked though solidarity means more than simply voting together in the House. Party discipline depends just as critically on caucus secrecy. A caucus can appear united only when any dissension is left inside the room once a caucus meeting has ended. And only in the seclusion of caucus can the governing party afford the luxury of dissension.

The strength of party discipline is directly and positively related to the government's use of confidence. The more often a government treats votes as matters as confidence, the more it must insist that its backbench vote with the government. Party discipline is necessary only when a government believes (or lets others believe) that it will have to go to the people – hold an election – if it loses a vote in the House. The problem therefore is not party discipline itself but rather overuse of confidence. And in most Canadian legislatures, confidence has become the single commandment of parliamentary life.

For party leaders in both opposition and government the question is how to sustain party discipline. One way is loyalty. Party leaders try to reward loyalty to themselves and the party (Mellon 1993, 4). Given the relatively weak advantage that incumbency offers most members at election time, this type of loyalty is not difficult to engender. Most members arrive in Ottawa based on the popularity of their leader and their party. The minimal personal vote in Canada (both federally and provincially) means that members' careers are heavily dependent on their leader. Rookie members of Parliament cannot expect much more than a 5 percent boost from their own reputations (Docherty 1997, 213). Veteran members can hope perhaps to double that cushion. But as the Conservative sweep to power in 1984 taught the Liberals, and as the Liberal sweep in 1993 instructed the Conservatives, even cabinet ministers with national reputations cannot withstand large swings against their party.

When loyalty does not work, leaders can turn to sanctions. Leaders in opposition have few immediate sanctions available. The threat of not having a critic portfolio (if the caucus outnumbers the cabinet) can and has been used. A more substantial threat (or advance sanction) is the understanding that should the party form the government, a wayward member will never sit in cabinet. For the government party, the available sanctions are far more numerous. Members can be relieved of any of their government, party, or parliamentary positions including cabinet, parliamentary secretary, whip, House leader, deputy whip or House leader, or sought-after committee spots. Usually, the mere threat of removal is enough to sustain party discipline. If necessary, however, members can be asked to leave caucus.

The ultimate federal sanction is for party leaders simply not to sign a member's nomination papers. The Canada Elections Act requires that party leaders sign the papers of any member running under the party banner. If the nomination is not signed, the candidate cannot use the party name on signs, literature, and most importantly, the ballot. The need for strong sanctions in Canada has been limited, in large part because members observe party discipline in most matters.

Since 1997 there has been increased resistance to party discipline. The seeds of this rebellion were sown in the 1993 federal campaign and came from both the government and opposition backbenches. The mantra of the Reform Party of Canada (and from 2000 to 2003 the Canadian Alliance) centred on changing the nature of representation in the Commons. Specifically, the party ran on the need for members to represent constituent views over the views of their party and leader. In addition, the Liberal campaign manifesto in 1993, the Red Book, pledged to free members from restrictive party whips (Liberal Party 1993, 92).

However, despite promises heading into the 1993 national vote, the thirty-fifth Parliament saw a rather stringent dependence on party discipline. On the Liberal side of the House this was due to Prime Minister Chrétien's willingness to consider almost every government vote a matter of confidence (Thomas 1998). Included among these votes was the famous Bill C-68 gun control legislation, which forced many rural backbench Liberal MPs to choose between their party and their constituents. Most chose the former, though nine Liberals did break with their colleagues and vote against the legislation (Docherty 1997, 165). Many were punished for their actions.

For the Reform Party, the experience of the thirty-fifth Parliament was no less troubling. In many ways the Reform Party had run for office by running against Parliament. Their standard bearers were individuals who did not like being politicians but wanted to be elected. Parliament was broken and the Reform Party was going to fix it, primarily by relaxing party discipline and voting according to constituency wishes. Yet members of the Reform Party tended to vote as consistently as any of the other parties did. This was later just as true of the Canadian Alliance. Why? For one, members of the Reform/Alliance shared small-c conservative principles such as lower taxes, smaller government, and a larger military. On most matters there was little need for dissension. Even in matters of conscience, most Alliance MPs' consciences were in unison. This unity of principle has been true of New Democrats as well, though they have been less vocal about relaxing party discipline.

Second, members of the Reform caucus soon learned what many veteran MPs had long understood. On all but the most controversial and well-discussed issues, it is difficult to discern what the majority of constituents believe. Members do not have the resources to conduct scientific polls on all of the issues they must vote upon. Some members have conducted polls, but even they admit that this is the excep-

Table 7.3

Does party discipline stop MPs from actively representing constituents?

	Personally (%)	How my colleagues would answer this question (%)
A great deal	5.9	18.8
Somewhat	40.0	42.5
Not very much	43.5	36.3
Not at all	10.6	2.5
Total (N)	100.0 (85)	100.1 (80)

Source: Author's survey of MPs, 2001.

tion (Docherty 1997, 166). On the majority of issues, members hear only from those constituents with very strong views, and quite often these views are polar opposites. This phenomenon is not new, but it was a surprise to many new Reform MPs (ibid.).

By the thirty-seventh Parliament, many members of the class of 1993 had acquired a more nuanced understanding of representation. After first coming to office thinking that party discipline was a barrier to effective local representation, many now understood that the lion's share of representation is undertaken outside of the chamber. Party whips may be unpleasant, but they rarely affect questions of local representation. Over half of all surveyed MPs thought party discipline had little to no impact on their ability to represent their voters (see Table 7.3). However, this evidence must be placed in its proper context. While less than 6 percent said it hampered them a great deal, nearly 19 percent thought it was an obstacle for their colleagues. In fact, just over 40 percent of surveyed members felt that party discipline at least somewhat hampered the ability of their peers to actively represent their constituents. The higher numbers may actually be a closer reflection of reality, as many MPs might be hesitant, even in an anonymous survey, to admit that they cannot represent their constituents. If so, then close to two-thirds of all members see whipped votes as a threat to active representation.

No wonder, then, that despite a growing appreciation of the subtleties of representation, there is still strong support for relaxing party

Table 7.4

Support for more free votes

	MPs (%)	MLAs (%)
Strongly support	45.2	38.9
Support with qualifications	44.0	45.9
Don't really support	8.3	9.2
Don't support at all	2.4	5.9
Total (N)	99.9 (84)	99.9 (185)

Sources: Author's surveys of MPs, 2001, and MLAs, 2002.

discipline and holding more free votes. As Table 7.4 indicates, support for more free votes is just as solid provincially as it is federally.

By 2000 most Alliance MPs had come to understand that relaxing party discipline, while still a strong goal, was a more complex issue than originally thought. At the same time, the Liberal Party was beginning its third consecutive majority, and many backbench members of the government, now seven-year parliamentary veterans, realized that as long as Jean Chrétien was prime minister, their chances of sitting in cabinet were next to nonexistent. The threat of sanctions seemed to lose much of its power.

The prime minister's impending retirement, a strong cohort of leadership support for Finance Minister Paul Martin (soon to lose that position), and Liberal backbenchers who felt their input was being ignored eventually coalesced over the most unlikely of issues, the selection process for committee chairs (Docherty 2004). In November 2002 the Canadian Alliance introduced a motion calling for the secret election of committee chairs (Francoli and Scandiffio 2002). Some observers might consider secret votes antidemocratic; after all, the election of committee chairs should be transparent. However, open votes had been used by an overly dictatorial leader's office to force backbenchers into supporting candidates that might not have been their first choice (Persichilli 2002). Secret votes meant that Liberal backbenchers would actually gain some independence from the leader's office.

Table 7.5

Impact of free votes on government

	House of Commons			Provincial and territorial assemblies		
	Total (%)	Government (%)	Opposition (%)	Total (%)	Government (%)	Opposition (%)
Lose only one or two	8.4	12.2	5.3	8.0	14.5	4.1
Could govern but be weaker	34.9	53.7	15.8	46.3	55.7	20.4
Could continue to govern	56.6	34.1	78.9	45.7	29.5	75.5
Total (N)	100.0 (83)	100.0 (41)	100.0 (38)	100.0 (175)	100.0 (61)	100.0 (49)

Sources: Author's surveys of MPs, 2001, and MLAs, 2002.

It was not surprising that the motion passed (all opposition parties favoured it). The size of the rebellion – fifty-six Liberals sided with the opposition – was more impressive. It is rare for votes on procedural matters to be the subject of front-page news. Given the prime minister's impending retirement, the resistance was seen as a further blow to Chretien's leadership and a boost to Paul Martin (McCarthy 2002c; Docherty 2004). The opposition was tempted to tap into this sentiment by suggesting the government was in disarray and not capable of governing. Had they done so, they would have increased the incentive for governments to keep the whips as strong as possible.

Table 7.5 highlights the reason for the impasse in increasing the number of free votes in Canadian legislatures. The answer to the question of why governments do not have more free votes on issues not considered matters of confidence rests with the members themselves. Members of Parliament and provincial legislators were asked what the impact on a government would be if it had some legislation defeated on free votes. As the first column in the table indicates, the majority of federal members thought the government could continue to govern with little to no impact. There was slightly less support for this notion among MLAs.

However, once these percentages are broken down by government versus opposition status, larger differences emerge. Only one-third of

Liberal MPs thought they could continue to govern effectively after losing legislative votes in the Commons, even on matters that were not considered confidence in the government. This contrasts to nearly 80 percent of opposition respondents who thought a government would not be weakened. Part of the reason for strong party discipline stems from the views of those very members who have been chafing at the prime ministerial bit. They are afraid to be seen as weak, and they think strength is best illustrated by strong support of all government legislation, no matter how minor. The provincial breakdowns are almost identical. Opposition MLAs were more confident that the government could maintain its strength than government MLAs. Over half of the government MLAs felt that they might continue to govern but in a weaker state. Less than one-third thought that they could continue to govern unfettered, while just over three-quarters of opposition members held this view.

What hope is there for increased free votes, and a move toward the British three-line whip (as discussed in Chapter 3) in Canadian legislatures? The federal vote on selecting committee chairs brought an increased sense of strength in the backbenches of Canada. Lost in much of the discussion was the fact that the Liberal Party was still in government. At the end of the day, all that changed was the method of selecting committee chairs. Increasing the number of nonwhipped votes and relaxing the confidence convention in Canadian assemblies can work to remove some of the barriers to participation and allow members to more actively represent constituents.

But the success of relaxed confidence will depend on two things. First, governments must convince their own members that they can lose legislation, have a quick vote of confidence in the government, and then move on as if nothing had happened. The largest group of skeptics resides in the government backbenches. Second, governments must hold the opposition parties to their word and views, namely that defeat on legislation cannot be interpreted as a sign of a weak government.

This second requirement may be harder to fulfill, particularly at the federal level. After years on the opposition side of the House, members of some parties will be tempted to portray a government that loses a vote as weak. But taking on the democratic deficit by lessening party discipline requires the cooperation of all parties. This is as true in provincial and territorial capitals as it is in Ottawa. Separating the results of votes on isolated pieces of legislation from the larger question of confidence in the government is the crucial first step. A new understanding of confidence is the prerequisite to relaxing party discipline.

Catalysts for Constructive Participation: Hope Lies in Committees

The importance of committees in the legislative process cannot be understated. When observers of Canadian legislatures talk of meaningful reform, many point to the committee system as the most likely vehicle for reforming the assembly and the role of its members. This view is shared by many legislators, who see committees as having many strengths and the potential to be even more valuable. The reasons for this are straightforward.

First, committees operate outside the more formal atmosphere and media glare of the chamber. Members tend to approach committee work in a more relaxed mood; there is often less overt partisan tension, and members work cooperatively (even if cooperation is just among the opposition parties). Second, committees are more directly engaged in policy discussions than the legislature as a whole. Both standing and legislative committees deal with concrete policy issues. In the chamber, bills and motions are debated, but the details are discussed less than the principles surrounding the issue. In committees, the details and the principles are all on the table, offering greater opportunity for meaningful discussion.

Third, and as a direct result of the first two reasons, committees encourage specialization. Members tend to serve on committees that overlap their local and critic responsibilities. As a result, members tend to have a greater understanding of the issues, and the problems surrounding the issues, that they are dealing with in committees.

Consequently they are less inclined to reduce debate to lowest common denominators (partisan heckling) and more inclined to convince through informed discussion and debate.

Fourth, committees enjoy some very important powers. While their authority is derived from the legislature, and therefore they are only as strong as the chamber permits them to be, they do exercise great control over those areas they have authority to investigate and particularly over witnesses. In fact, as long as a committee is investigating something within its prescribed authority, it has almost unlimited powers not only to call any witness but also to demand any documents it determines relevant to its inquiry (Davidson 1995, 12). In fact, a committee's authority to demand responses from witnesses it has called is greater than that of the courts. In the words of the general legal counsel for the House of Commons, "There are legally no grounds upon which a witness can refuse to answer a question" (quoted ibid., 13). For legislators who see themselves suffering under the millstone of party discipline in the chamber, this power truly makes them masters of their own domain.

Fifth and finally, in Ottawa and the provinces, committees are staffed with employees of the legislature. That is, they have nonpartisan support staffs. In many cases these include clerks, who oversee procedure, and researchers, who provide nonpartisan analysis of the relevant policy issues. Within committees, members, and not political parties, rule.

For all the above reasons, many politicians place a great deal of faith in the committee process. However, committees in Canadian legislatures are not without their problems. Much of the exasperation felt by elected officials can be traced to the gap that exists between the potential of the committee system and the reality of committee work. Committees are not used effectively by governments and often only when the executive finds itself overburdened with responsibilities. Committees are seen as vehicles not for increasing participation but rather for solving short-term problems.

Committees in legislatures come in various forms, though most serve the same basic functions. The House of Commons has standing committees, legislative committees, special committees, and joint committees (with the Senate). Standing committees are given authority by the House to examine matters that are referred to them by the House or by statute or the standing orders. They are also the committees that examine most legislation; they hold public hearings, and debate and amend the legislation during the clause-by-clause process. While standing committees are formed for the duration of a Parliament, legislative committees are formed only to examine specific legislation. They cease to exist after the legislation has passed Parliament. Special committees, like legislative committees, exist only for specific purposes. Legislatures do not use them often, and usually for high-profile issues. They can be thought of as parliamentary task forces or mini royal commissions.

In some Parliaments, most notably under Prime Minister Mulroney, legislative committees have been used more widely, freeing up standing committees to engage in broader examinations of government policy. During this time, committees began "initiating many of their own inquiries" into departmental functions (Marleau 2000, 24). Committees were producing reports and examinations that the executive had not asked for. It was hardly surprising that the government systematically ignored these reports, but committee members grew increasingly frustrated. The Chrétien government reverted to the past practice of using standing committees to examine legislation. During the thirty-sixth Parliament, only Bill C-20, the Clarity Act, went to a legislative committee. All other bills were studied by standing committees.

Provinces and territories tend to follow the pattern of their federal colleagues. Ad hoc or special committees are rare (see Table 7.6). The Northwest Territories uses special committees more than most, and New Brunswick and Saskatchewan often turn to special committees, but most legislatures do not regularly form such bodies.

Unfortunately, many governments are just as likely to step outside the boundaries of the legislature and form committees comprised solely of their own members. These committees, or "task forces," can make reports directly to a minister. During the thirty-seventh Parliament of Canada there were no special committees. However, an all-Liberal task force was created to examine problems facing Canadian

Table 7.6

Resources and powers of committees

Jurisdiction	Staff resources (beyond clerk and technical)	Ad hoc/special committees	Can standing committees set own agenda?
House of Commons	Researcher and other assistance as required	Rare (only one in 36th Parliament)	Requires approval from the legislature, in legislation, or in standing orders
Newfoundland and Labrador	Public Accounts has researcher	Rare (two in past five years)	Requires formal approval from legislature
Prince Edward Island	Need permission to hire researcher	Rare (two in past six years)	Yes, by majority vote in committee
Nova Scotia	None	Rare (approximately one every two years)	Broad authority set out in standing orders
New Brunswick	Researchers retained as required	Quite frequently (two or more a year)	Requires formal approval from legislature
Quebec	Some have researchers	Rare (two in past ten years)	Yes
Ontario	One researcher per committee; lawyer for clause-by-clause examination of bills	Occasionally (one every two to three years)	Broad authority set out in standing orders
Manitoba	None	Very rare (none in past five years)	Requires formal approval from legislature
Saskatchewan	Assembly staff can be seconded and researchers hired	Common (approximately one per year)	Requires formal approval from legislature
Alberta	None	Rare (one in past three years)	Yes, within fixed budget
British Columbia	Three researchers for four committees	Approximately one per session	Requires formal approval from legislature
Northwest Territories	Researchers as required	Very common (three or four per session)	Broad authority set out in standing orders
Nunavut	One researcher per committee	Only one thus far	Yes
Yukon	None	Rare (one in last ten years)	Yes, by majority vote in committee

Sources: Author's survey of provincial and territorial legislative clerks, 2002; House of Commons 2001, c. 2.

urban areas and produced a major report on the state of Canadian cities and the role the federal government should play in addressing urban problems (known informally as the Sgro Report). Ontario also formed more government-member-only committees in the period 1999-2002 than it did all-party special committees.

From a government perspective the attractiveness of stepping outside the legislature but still using some elected officials is obvious. The committee has the appearance of elected officials participating in the policy process and reaching out to the public. Indeed, many of these government committee initiatives travel throughout the province or country to solicit public input. Meanwhile the likelihood of significant dissension within the committee is diminished because all the players are on the same team. Governments can also more tightly control the agenda and possible outcome of any report that is produced. If the findings of the committee are critical of government policy, the government is not in the embarrassing position of having an all-party committee take aim at its plans.

The problem with government-member-only task forces is a lack of both participation and representation. Because the task force is not a creature of the legislature, it has no established and transparent standards to follow. There is no requirement to hear from witnesses, to have open hearings, or to publish a report. Nor is it clear that all interested individuals and groups have equal access to make presentations (oral or written) to the committee. No nonpartisan employee of the legislature serves as clerk. In the absence of these resources it is difficult to distinguish between a government member task force and a partisan political exercise.

By contrast, committees of the legislature (standing, special, or legislative) may seem more divided and difficult to constrain, but they have the credibility that comes with being a creation of the legislature. One indication of the independence all-party committees enjoy is the level of resources they are provided with (see Table 7.6). All legislatures provide their committees with a clerk, who furnishes both procedural advice and organizational assistance. Among provincial legislatures, Ontario provides the most resources: each standing committee is provided with its own researcher and legal counsel when required. Nunavut legislators also enjoy a researcher for each committee. The role of committee researchers is vital. They take their direction, not from the legislature and the government House leader, but from the committee. Committees with researchers have greater freedom to choose what to investigate, as well as to control the depth and breadth of their research.

Of perhaps more concern to the question of committee independence is the varying ability that committees enjoy to establish their own parameters of investigation or their own agendas. In most cases, the committee mandate is established quite specifically either through the standing orders or through motions passed (typically by majority governments working under party discipline) in the legislative chamber. Although this necessarily limits the capability of committees to determine their sphere of investigation, this restriction has a positive aspect. As long as there is no requirement for the executive to respond to committee reports, the only ones they will pay serious attention to are those that they have requested. In other words, special committees, or standing committees charged with specific responsibilities by the legislature, have the best likelihood of their reports meeting a positive response from the executive.

As Table 7.7 indicates, few committees enjoy the legislative authority to force the executive to respond to their reports. This lack of authority is telling. Why should legislators spend time and effort hearing from witnesses, requesting research, and travelling across the country to produce reports that can easily be shelved? Six legislatures allow committees to demand or request responses. But there is no requirement that the recommendations of the committee actually be implemented, even if the committee report represents an all-party consensus.

Finally, it is interesting to note the relationship between committees of the legislature and officers and agencies that report to the legislature. One of the more significant reforms to take place in some assemblies in the mid-1980s provided committees with the power either to interview or to recommend the nominees for officers of the assembly. This reform was undertaken in the hope of a more significant role for committees in the selection process, and an improved working relationship between committees and agencies. These goals have not been clearly achieved. In some instances, dominant government majorities on committees virtually stack the deck in favour of an appointee who has the premier's or prime minister's blessing. In addition, competition

Table 7.7

Committee powers with respect to executive and officers of the house

Jurisdiction	Does government respond to committee reports within specified time?	Do committees interview or approve officers of House (auditor, etc.)?
House of Commons	Yes, if requested	Yes
Newfoundland and Labrador	No	No, but committees are consulted
Prince Edward Island	Must respond but timing varies	Committees recommend appointments
Nova Scotia	No	No
New Brunswick	No	Yes, as authorized by assembly
Quebec	No	No
Ontario	Yes, committee can request response within 120 days	Requires authorization but occurs routinely
Manitoba	No	Yes, different committees for different officers
Saskatchewan	Yes, committee can request response within 120 days	Provincial auditor only
Alberta	No	Search committees recommend appointments
British Columbia	No	Special committees appointed to select officers (not clerk of assembly)
Northwest Territories	Yes, committee can request response within 120 days	Only in an ad hoc fashion
Nunavut	Yes, within 120 days	Yes
Yukon	No	Speaker and all leaders participate in selection

Sources: Author's survey of provincial and territorial legislative clerks, 2002; Parliament of Canada, <www.parl.gc.ca>

continues between committees and agencies over the turf of accountability. Once appointed, officers of Parliament may report to a committee of the chamber, but they do not take direction from it. For example, if a Public Accounts Committee of a legislature cannot direct the auditor general to investigate particular departments or programs, having a hand in his or her selection may be of minimal benefit.

At the same time, this power to participate in the selection process allows committees to question potential officers about their understanding of the role of committees, members, and agencies in the scrutiny function. At the very least this serves an educative function for incoming officers. They have the opportunity to understand how members value the work of committees, and the frustrations that members face while performing their accountability functions. Potential officers also witness the important informal workings of parliamentary committees. The tangible benefits of such an experience are difficult to quantify, but denying committees any involvement holds more obvious problems. Bodies engaged in the scrutiny function, be they committees of the House or officers of the House, should have an appreciation of each other's duties. When this is not the case, the prospects for effective accountability are further diminished.

Conclusion

Of the three functions of elected assemblies, the legislative task faces the most challenges, primarily challenges of participation and responsiveness. The trick in successful governance is to balance the need for participation of all members of the assembly with the constitutional requirement that governments be able to proceed with their legislative agendas. When governments allow for greater participation from all members, they are also addressing the question of responsiveness. For when members can participate inside the legislature, they are responding to the needs of the citizens they were elected to represent.

The speech from the throne offers some opportunity for participation from government backbench members. It would be folly to suggest that matters that are raised in the throne speech should not be considered matters of confidence. After all, many throne speeches are a précis of the campaign platform. However, when governments open new legislative sessions with throne speeches full of pledges that might not be based on strong input from the caucus, the ability of members to participate and respond openly and freely is greatly compromised. The difficulty with the throne speech is the lack of institutional avenues for member participation before it is read.

The same was once true of budgets. If members had the ability to participate it was far from transparent. Budget secrecy and the lack of an open consultation process meant that budgets – and therefore the annual economic policy of the government – were left in the hands of the minister of finance, the prime minister, and a select few in the inner circle. Many jurisdictions have seen recent and noticeable improvements in budgetary procedures. Federally, the end of budget secrecy has dramatically opened up the process. Prebudget consultations and an all-party committee report have allowed greater participation on two fronts: members and the public have been brought into the process. Elected representatives on an all-party prebudget committee can play a proactive role in recommending fiscal and social policies to the minister of finance. Interested citizens and organizations can express their views on the record. This is not a trivial matter. Further, using a committee of the assembly, as opposed to a one-party committee, signals that most groups should find at least one set of sympathetic ears on the committee.

The importance of committees cannot be overemphasized, but unfortunately they are underutilized. Too many jurisdictions in Canada are reluctant to use committees to their full effectiveness. The result is to severely limit the ability of members to participate in legislative functions. Prelegislative scrutiny of bills, whereby committees can hear from witnesses and discuss legislation before being locked into the principles of government policy, provides a real possibility to engage citizens on matters of public policy. By the time legislation receives second reading approval, governments are less willing to compromise, even in the face of strong opposition. The success of prelegislative scrutiny in other jurisdictions (and in its sporadic use in Canada) suggests we should look seriously at this option.

Finally, citizens, politicians, and academic observers are tempted to think of party discipline as the greatest single constraint on responsiveness. Remove party discipline and members can properly represent their constituents. Certainly Canadian assemblies have tended to treat party discipline as an unalterable part of parliamentary democracy. But Canadian legislatures can afford to treat fewer items of legislation as matters of confidence in the government. The introduction of a British three-line whip system would go some way to improving the ability of members to respond to constituents.

Yet there is more to party discipline than freedom for government members. Any moves to allow more free votes would have to be treated very seriously by opposition parties. Governments will experiment with traditional Canadian understandings of confidence only if it does not compromise their ability to govern effectively. The most effective method of dealing with the question of confidence is to be very clear about the status of bills upon their introduction. Changing gears on confidence because a bill might be losing support only signals inconsistency, and opposition parties cannot help but exploit any perceived weaknesses. But if new legislation is clearly marked as a matter upon which the government's future does not rest, then the government should not lose any credibility if the bill is defeated. In addition, this change might allow legislative and standing committees more freedom to offer innovative proposals to such a bill during public hearings and clause-by-clause reading. This can only serve to improve participation and responsiveness.

Chapter 7

Strengths

✦ The speech from the throne and budget debates are prime examples of government responsiveness. At its best, the former reiterates campaign pledges and establishes the government's legislative agenda. The latter outlines the government's fiscal policies and responds to the economic and social challenges of the day.

✦ Canadian legislators agree that party discipline should be relaxed. Yet most elected officials state that present levels of discipline do not diminish their ability to represent their constituents.

✦ The best hope for increasing meaningful participation within legislative assemblies lies in reform of the committee system. Sending legislation to committees immediately after first reading provides committees with greater scope to alter bills' contents.

Weaknesses

✦ Many jurisdictions rely too heavily on closure and time allocation. This reliance may be a sign that political parties cannot agree on the balance between allowing a government to move forward with its agenda and the need for the opposition to scrutinize government plans.

✦ Canadian legislators do not agree on the potential effect of less party discipline on the ability of a government to function properly. Government members are more wary of increased free votes (and of losing votes) than are opposition members.

✦ Canadian legislatures do not take a uniform approach to how legislation is handled in committees. As a result, there are mixed opportunities for Canadians to present evidence to committees.

8 WHAT LEGISLATURES SHOULD (AND SHOULD NOT) DO

Much of the argument presented in this audit suggests that legislatures and legislators are increasingly overburdened. The combination of rules and resources has created barriers to effective participation and responsiveness. But many legislators have overcome the obstacles to good governance and managed to respond to the concerns of voters.

Canadian legislators and legislatures face many challenges in the twenty-first century. Too many of our legislatures do not have enough members to perform their scrutiny function properly. Too many legislatures are not meeting often enough or allowing for greater debate. The number of sitting days is too low, and the use of closure or time allocation sends the wrong message to the public. Committees have great potential, but are too often underutilized. Many committees do not reach out enough, and do not travel or hear from witnesses during the study of legislation. This comes at the direct cost of participation and responsiveness.

This concluding chapter begins with a brief discussion of the largest single challenge facing legislatures in Canada: the perception that elected assemblies are losing relevance. This notion only plays into the hands of governments happy to escape the accountability mechanisms of Westminster democracies. The several options for reforming legislatures presented here are neither unique nor revolutionary. Wide-ranging changes will not necessarily improve the democratic performance of legislatures. Those who call for sweeping reforms should be warned that they may not end up with the type of assembly they were hoping for. Giving all members too much authority to initiate legislation and policy might prevent government from responding to citizens. The trick is to offer changes that lead to greater participation without introducing the possibility of US congressional-style gridlock.

Legislatures and the Problem of Relevance

The attempt by the Ontario government in the spring of 2003 to introduce a budget outside the precincts of the assembly illustrates the problems faced by many legislatures. The government of Ernie Eves decided that the budget could be read to a studio audience and broadcast live via satellite and Internet. The stated rationale, to reach out to more people in the province, seemed designed to draw attention away from the government's plans to avoid the legislature. The premier and his colleagues were clearly hoping the public would not notice. Eves himself stated that the only people who might get upset were the opposition, the press gallery, and a few professors (Mackie 2003a).

The reaction against this move must have surprised those who thought it would be an innovative way to reach citizens without using the legislative process. Much of the opposition did come from the press and professors, but there was also strong opposition from within the premier's own party. The outgoing speaker of the assembly charged that the premier was listening to backroom advisors and not his elected caucus (Mackie 2003b). He opined that the premier was making the legislature irrelevant, and he was absolutely right.

The culprit was not the rank-and-file members of the legislature, but rather the cabinet that was actively trying to avoid scrutiny. If legislatures are becoming irrelevant it is because governments want them to be. Cabinets benefit when legislatures meet less often. The increasing trend toward fewer sitting days, more announcements outside the chamber, and "speaking directly to the people" by avoiding institution-alized opposition is the single largest threat to representative democ-racy. Shorter sessions, closure and time allocation, omnibus legislation, and budgets delivered in infomercial fashion are direct attempts to avoid scrutiny.

Canadians elect 308 members to represent us in the House of Com-mons. At most 15 percent are chosen to serve in cabinet. These individuals are properly held to account only by the government backbench and the opposition parties. When cabinets avoid these watchdogs, they avoid being accountable for their actions. Institutionalized scrutiny in Westminster systems is the equivalent to the checks and balances in US congressional-style governments. Canada's representative democ-racy was based on conservative values of trust in authority and does not provide different branches of government with overlapping author-ity. It is very efficient government. Our system provides cabinet gov-ernment with amazing resources to govern, but with this power comes responsibility. Governors (prime ministers and premiers) must be will-ing to answer for their actions. The strength of our system is that it requires the executive to answer unscripted questions. They cannot duck their duties unless they go out of their way to avoid the legisla-ture. While the Ontario government's March 2003 budget decision was perhaps the most egregious transgression of accountability, it is not the only one.

In order for legislatures to be relevant, all members of assemblies must be willing to abide by the rules of the chamber. For members of the cabinet, these rules should include attendance requirements. In addition, cabinet members should be obliged to make major policy announcements inside the assembly and not in staged photo opportu-nities across the country. Speakers consistently urge ministers to follow such practices but have little power to enforce them. They should become part of the standard operating procedure of legislative assemblies.

Some provinces have instituted financial penalties on cabinet min-isters who do not meet spending targets. The Ontario Taxpayer Protec-tion Act imposes salary cuts to ministers in times of deficit budgets.

This accountability is self-defined by those who are making the decisions. There are no penalties for ministers who refuse to be held to account for their policy choices. Consequently this audit recommends stricter attendance rules. Legislatures should meet more often and members of the executive should be required to attend at least 80 percent of question periods. Anything short of that indicates a failure to live up to their accountability requirements.

In the eyes of the cabinet, attendance requirements may give undue access to members of the opposition to criticize the government. But this is how the Westminster system of government was designed to function: the government must respond to opposition calls for accountability. Further, given the resources available to the government, question period is hardly a threat to the cabinet's ability to see its legislative agenda through. Although question period tends to favour the opposition, government backbenchers also participate in this process. Requiring attendance of cabinet ministers could result in executives listening to their own backbench more closely, even if the questions are less challenging than opposition queries. Majority governments could still govern successfully.

Governments must be transparent and accountable. The venue for this accountability is the legislative assembly and its associated committees. Legislatures can be relevant only if politicians – and in particular cabinet ministers – are willing to face institutionalized scrutiny. Further reforms, also aimed at improving the relevance of legislatures, follow.

Increasing the Size of Legislatures

Addressed specifically in Chapter 6, the problem of the size of some legislatures was a theme throughout this audit. Determining the proper size of a legislature is an impossible task, and advocating more politicians is an unpopular argument. Nevertheless, many assemblies in Canada should be larger. We can begin with understanding the two extremes. We could move toward direct democracy, wherein everybody represents themselves. This is mirror representation without the mirror. Of course, in modern society this is just not practical. On the other extreme we could elect one person alone to represent us. The entire country would be a single-member district. This too is impractical, because it entails no accountability. Electing one individual is blank-cheque government.

Of course no modern democratic society would choose either of those extremes; somewhere between them lies representative government. However, these two absolutes show that a significant increase in the size of a legislature might not represent a considerable change. While there is no perfect size for a legislature, the number of elected officials should be a function of two considerations: the population that needs to be represented and the duties that need to be performed.

In terms of population, Canadian legislatures run the gamut from the House of Commons, representing over 30 million people, to Nunavut, representing just over 26,000. Obviously the former requires more members than the latter, but not over a thousand times more. We must also remember that parliamentary legislatures include the executive, and this has a direct impact on the size of an assembly. In terms of the duties to be performed, there is a difference between members of the executive and other members of the legislature. Members of cabinet do not actively engage in many legislative functions. They do not serve on committees, they do not ask questions in the chamber, and they do not hold government to account. Instead, they send legislation to committees, answer questions in the House, and ideally are held accountable by other members.

In particularly small assemblies, such as Prince Edward Island's with twenty-seven members, a cabinet may consist of almost half of the elected officials. This taxes the resources of those charged with the accountability function, who must also serve their constituents. Their ability to fully participate in all their tasks is compromised. In New Brunswick, where many surveyed MLAs reported inadequate constituency resources, the problem can be even more severe. These members must choose between representation and responsiveness in the riding, or scrutiny and participation in the legislative arena.

Chapter 6 found that only in the federal House of Commons is the ratio of cabinet ministers to private members greater than one to four. Ideally, a legislature should be at least four times the size of the cabinet. This would allow a legislature to hold a full cabinet, a complete cohort of parliamentary secretaries, a large caucus, and at least one opposition party whose members had no more than one critic portfolio each. This is a minimum. Larger assemblies would have members who could concentrate much of their energy on committee work. In jurisdictions where multiple parties compete and regularly have official party status (the House of Commons, Quebec, Ontario, Manitoba) larger assemblies would allow greater participation by different interests. Most provincial assemblies could easily withstand a 50 percent increase in size. The House of Commons would not suffer from a one-third growth in members.

Of course all of this is moot in cases such as British Columbia in the 2001 election, when the government won seventy-seven of seventy-nine seats. The landslide would have been even larger with fewer districts. As John Courtney (2004) explains in his volume of this Audit series, single-member plurality electoral systems exaggerate victory. Winning parties consistently win a greater percentage of seats than they do votes. The smaller the assembly, the greater this embellishment. More districts would help minimize this distortion. And even when a large sweep reduces the elected opposition to little more than a rearguard, there is nothing unhealthy or even undemocratic about an ample government backbench keeping its own ministers on the straight and narrow.

Even though the House of Commons surpasses the one to four ratio, it could be significantly enlarged. The incremental growth of the House based on the decennial census could be supplemented with a substantial fillip. There would be a number of benefits to such a move (Franks 1987, 267). First, smaller districts would mean closer contact with voters. Members might be able to build a personal profile that would allow them to withstand swings against their party. At present there are no rewards for local service, just potential risks for ignoring this work. Smaller constituencies might allow members to build name recognition independent of their party.

Second, a larger Commons might more easily permit freer votes. Based on the British experience, large majorities provide greater flexibility on party discipline. Government backbenchers can "twin" with opposition members to neutralize the effect of each voting against the party. Alternatively, government private members understand that they can vote against their party without compromising the ability of the government to pass its legislation. The larger the assembly, the greater the likelihood that governments can withstand a modest degree of rebellion.

The third and greatest result of a substantially larger Commons would be to diminish the attraction of a seat at the cabinet table. Canadian assemblies lack a critical mass of parliamentarians. Instead, the rows of the government backbenches are filled with members hoping for an eventual cabinet seat. Across the floor, the ambitions are very similar: most opposition members assume they are only a victory away from a car with driver and the ability to initiate legislation. Few MPs see a parliamentary career as a desirable goal. One method of making it more desirable is simply to make it more realistic. For example, in Britain the large Commons (over 650 MPs) means that most members soon understand they will never be in cabinet. As a result, many turn their attention to the scrutiny function. They become true parliamentarians, engaged in participation and responsiveness through the chamber, and less beholden to their leader. Private members become policy experts who develop loyalty to a committee system. And because of their numbers, they can devote greater attention to only one committee, thus reinforcing their expertise in a chosen policy field.

The Canadian House of Commons does not have to double in size. But increasing the number of ridings could potentially address some of the present problems with inclusiveness. Chambers in Canada have made progress in the past decades, but are still far from reflective of the people they represent. Smaller districts, at both the federal and provincial levels, might allow constituencies to more accurately reflect demographic communities of interest. There is no downside to a more inclusive, reflective chamber.

The final note with respect to size relates to official party status. Different legislatures have different rules determining this status: the House of Commons uses a floor of twelve members, Ontario uses nine. But these numbers are random. In the case of the House of Commons it was thought that no party would have fewer than a dozen seats. We know that this is not the case. Yet parties are penalized for electing fewer than this pre-established number of members. They are not allowed to participate regularly in proceedings of the chamber, and their research funding is severely limited. Following the 2001 British Columbia election, the New Democratic Party was the only opposition – with two members. On top of the regular obstacles they faced in keeping the government accountable was the problem of resources. They were not given the caucus research funding that the Liberal backbench could draw upon.

Official party status should be automatic to the largest opposition party, no matter what its size. Further, official party status should be granted to parties that elect 5 percent of the members of an assembly. In the case of Prince Edward Island, this would mean a single elected member could have official party status and be allowed to ask questions and regularly participate. In the case of British Columbia, the second rule would not apply, but the first rule would give the two-member NDP official status.

There are costs to increasing legislative chambers. Elected members require staff, and the budgets of assemblies would naturally increase. The experience of Ontario is instructive, however. When its legislature was reduced, the cost per member rose. Not only did members demand higher salaries but the workload of the constituency office increased. Smaller constituencies may result in lower costs per office. But democracy is not cheap, and cost should not be the determining factor. The largest cost in a move to increase legislatures is the political one, which is substantial. In an era with little trust in public officials, a pledge to have more politicians is hardly politically attractive. However, Canadians could be made to understand that more politicians does not mean more spending or waste. Within our parliamentary system it means more accountability, more representation, and more responsiveness.

Resources to Ridings

The Audit found that most assemblies provide good constituency resources to their members, and members in turn provide good constituency services to citizens. In terms of responsiveness, Canadians are well served at the local level. Members of Parliament have up-to-date, well-supplied constituency offices. In more remote areas, additional funds are available to help MPs overcome the obstacles of distance and dispersed constituents.

Provincially, the resources provided to elected representatives vary. In Prince Edward Island, regional service centres are shared by more than one MLA. This efficient use of resources would be impractical in just about every other jurisdiction. Despite having the third-smallest average constituency population among all provinces, MLAs in New Brunswick have expressed some concern that they do not have the resources necessary to respond to constituents properly. Certainly they are less resourced than Nova Scotia MLAs, who on average have 25 percent more voters per district but receive a 48 percent larger budget for staff. No doubt some improvements could be made in all jurisdictions in terms of budgetary resources.

One freedom enjoyed by most elected officials is the ability to allocate their staff resources. Staff shortages in a constituency office are likely to be the result of a member's decision to increase capital staff at the cost of the district, and vice versa. This freedom recognizes that members are best positioned to determine the needs of their districts. Moreover, if members choose to ignore voters and concentrate all their resources in the capital, the legislature or party caucus does not wish to be held responsible. Staffing should be an individual choice, not a party or legislative decision.

A few concerns about constituency resources were found in this audit. Members have indicated that service cuts in government departments typically have implications for constituency offices (2001 MP survey). Most notable were the concerns of some urban members over the increasing demands on their offices for immigration assistance. Constituency staff are essentially caseworkers, but they cover many areas of expertise. Their work cannot be viewed in isolation from that of the broader public service. Therefore constituency offices (both at the federal and subnational level) must be plugged into program and policy changes in the capital. Constituency workers are the unsung heroes of representation and responsiveness. As such it is critical that they have access to the necessary resources to fulfill their functions.

One disturbing result of the Audit related to the Internet (see Chapter 4). The non-exhaustive survey of websites at the federal level, buttressed by other studies, found that few members of Parliament make good use of web resources. This is unfortunate as web technology provides an efficient and instructive vehicle for reaching constituents. Members are much slower than the public to use this technology, perhaps out of fear that websites diminish the role of constituency staff. But information provided on a member's website should supplement the role of the constituency office, not make it redundant. Members should be providing as much information as possible on the web, from how to solve common constituency problems to how to petition the Parliament of Canada.

Here the legislature needs to take some responsibility. The Parliament of Canada's website, for example, should provide direct links to its members' own sites, as the Senate website does. The few senators who have taken advantage of web technology have been innovative and imaginative. Many MPs (and MLAs) do use the Internet, but easily finding or accessing their websites can be difficult. Standardized URLs (differentiated by name only), supported by the Commons, would require some MPs to mute the partisan tone of their sites. MPs could, however, still maintain a separate partisan site. A website supported by the House of Commons would be monitored to ensure that it was not a political vehicle, much as members' regular mailings to constituents ("householders") are currently regulated. Such changes could also be implemented at the provincial and territorial level.

Finally, there is an argument that members are well resourced at the local level simply to encourage them to have a constituency, not legislative, focus. Indeed, members are encouraged to engage heavily in local service. But most members enjoy this type of work and see tangible results from helping voters or local groups. By contrast, much of the work done in the legislature is removed from concrete action. It is harder to make a difference in the Commons or a provincial assembly than it is to solve the concerns of an individual voter. But the response to this imbalance should be reforms that make it possible for members to have a greater impact in the legislative arena.

Positions in the House and Salaries

Chapter 3 argued that most positions in legislatures tend to reinforce the dominance of party over individual members. This is part of Canadian legislative life: parties dominate legislatures. At the same time, most legislatures have taken significant steps to ensure that members collectively understand their role and their ownership of the legislature.

The election of the speaker through a secret ballot is the single most important reform that Canadian legislatures have embraced in the past four decades. It has done more than simply provide the speaker with a sense of independence and legitimacy, although even this cannot be underestimated. More important, the change signals to premiers and prime ministers that all members of the assembly have an equal say in determining the leadership of the chamber. The fight in Ontario between Speaker Gary Carr and Premier Ernie Eves over the spring 2003 budget is telling. It is difficult for a speaker who has been selected by a premier to have the ability to stand up on behalf of the rights of all members of the legislature. Knowing he had been selected by a majority of all members gave the speaker the moral authority required to protect the interests of opposition and government members.

What Legislatures Should (and Should Not) Do

The process for choosing the speaker should be used as a model for selecting committee chairs. Because chairs serve all members of a committee, chairs should owe their allegiance and loyalty to their committee and not to the party in power. The change in procedures instituted in Ottawa in early 2003, over the objection of the government, provides committee chairs with the same independence the speaker enjoys. Other assemblies should follow this example. There is nothing untoward or undemocratic about a secret ballot election. Open votes for committee chairs serve only the interests of the party in power.

Further, while a political party must retain the authority to sanction its members, pulling members from committees based on actions unrelated to committee activity is a questionable practice. Members should understand that their membership on a parliamentary committee has some stability. At present in Ottawa, the party in power cannot overturn a vote on a committee chair. However, the party can remove the elected chair from the committee for the same net result. This audit recommends that committee assignments should be semipermanent. Members should leave the committee only of their own volition, or if their actions in the committee are at odds with the fundamental principles of their party. They should not be removed from a committee for voting against their party on one issue, whether that vote occurs in the committee or in the chamber.

Finally, the use of committee substitutes, necessary when members are stretched, often results in members voting or speaking on matters that they are ill prepared to debate. Committee substitution should be limited. Members should see their committee responsibilities as part of their legislative duties. Attendance at committees should be strongly encouraged and limits should be placed on the number of substitutions a party or member is allowed to make.

Most premiers and prime ministers enjoy total authority to select their cabinets. Chapter 3 suggested that members of Parliament are both more skeptical and more realistic than the public about the criteria used by prime ministers in selecting cabinets. Prime ministers often place ability and talent well down the list; loyalty to the leader is generally the number-one qualification for cabinet. However, changing

the selection process too dramatically might have unintended consequences. Prime ministers must expect loyalty from their executive,
and must enjoy some freedom to select the women and men who will
join them at the cabinet table. In fact, this freedom allows the prime
minister to make up for shortfalls in representation – regional or
demographic – that might have resulted from the vagaries of the electoral process. Cabinet selection through a system of seniority or caucus might exclude some areas of the country.

There is little to be gained by tying the hands of the prime minister
when it comes to the selection of cabinet ministers. When properly
chosen, cabinets can contain a broad variety of experience, and can
reflect as many faces of Canada as the legislature elects. When a cabinet is poorly selected, it is not reflective of Parliament but rather of the
premier or prime minister who did the choosing. The government will
pay the ultimate price for a poor cabinet with unpopular policies and
decisions. Taking the selection process out of their hands would only
remove their responsibility.

The head of government also selects the men and women who assist
ministers, which is not unexpected given the quasi-executive nature of
a parliamentary secretary. However, this position has failed to live up
to its billing. The evidence presented in Chapter 3 suggested that a parliamentary secretaryship is not the stepping stone to cabinet that
many individuals (including some prime ministers) claim it to be.
While some parliamentary secretaries eventually make it to cabinet,
most are demoted from their position before an eventual promotion to
a different task. The rotation of parliamentary secretaries creates an
illusory carrot for members. They are taught to think of this position
as preparation for cabinet and an inducement to strong party cohesion. The reality is that many members gain some policy experience
and then return to the backbenches of government. This is an unfortunate waste of parliamentary talent.

The Audit recommends that the position of parliamentary secretary
be made more akin to the British "junior ministers to assist" role. David
Hutchison (2000) has argued persuasively for the introduction of a two-
tier system of parliamentary secretaries. The tier one appointments

would serve as junior ministers. They would be expected to dedicate a great deal of their time to this function, which would be treated as an opportunity to demonstrate their potential to be full ministers of the Crown. These appointments would be limited to the larger departments, where ministers could use the assistance of two of their elected colleagues. A second tier would be available to all departments. As Hutchison explains, these positions might be given to rookie members of government as a way of introducing them to the policy process and providing them an opportunity to understand the interaction of Parliament and the machinery of government. Rotation in these latter posts would have less negative impact than it would in the former.

This proposal for two-tier parliamentary secretaryships is applicable only in the House of Commons. The size of provincial legislatures does not justify such a change, which would further deplete their resources. Even at the federal level, this reform makes sense only when tied to the earlier proposal of a larger House of Commons. The combination of a much larger House and defined roles for two sets of parliamentary secretaries would help clarify the accountability function for most members. Rookie MPs who served as junior parliamentary secretaries (as opposed to junior ministers) would understand at the beginning of their tenure that they will soon be back in the chamber performing their accountability function. There will be no false expectations of cabinet spots.

This Audit did not spend a great deal of time examining the role or impact of salaries of elected officials. However, this issue is worth exploring briefly. In every elected assembly in Canada, members of cabinet, parliamentary secretaries, whips, and deputies are provided additional salaries. These extra salaries also carry pension benefits. Salaries alone hardly act as an inducement to members to seek out cabinet and other positions of influence that reinforce party behaviour. However, additional salaries for ministerial and parliamentary secretary functions exceed most of the additional salaries geared toward the scrutiny function. The addition may be tied to the responsibilities, but it also further fosters loyalty to the leader. Demotion can have financial implications.

Members in positions that have a clearly legislative focus receive salary top-ups. These positions include the speaker, whips, House leaders, their deputies, and committee chairs. Until 2001 the federal House of Commons did not provide committee chairs with a salary top-up. At present the top-up for federal chair is 75 percent of a parliamentary secretary's. If only to signal the important role played by committees in the legislative process, committee chairs should have salaries that are at least commensurate with those of parliamentary secretaries.

Party Discipline

As discussed in the previous chapter, party discipline is the whipping boy of Canadian legislatures. Discipline is not a variable in the representation equation in Canada, but a constant. For leaders of governments it is a religion. For many government backbenchers it is both a blessing and a curse. Members of the populist Reform/Alliance experiment saw it as anathema to responsiveness. How can party cohesion be such an evil to some and the enabler of good governance to others?

Clearly party discipline, the need to vote as a unit, favours the government. Prime ministers encourage their caucus to treat most bills and motions as matters of confidence simply because it makes their lives easier. Like the cliché that majority governments in Canada are little more than elected dictatorships, attacks on party discipline by the opposition are banal. First, individuals with ideologically similar views, often elected from constituencies where the majority of voters share similar demographic features and political values, find it easy to criticize the need for government to command discipline from its members. For members of the Canadian Alliance and the New Democratic Party, voting their conscience has often been the same as voting the party line because of the ideological consistency within their ranks. Governing parties that straddle a broader spectrum of public opinion cannot rely on such natural unity of purpose. The newly created Conservative Party of Canada may find stronger ideological strains as it now represents a broader spectrum than the former Alliance or the Progressive Conservative Party.

In addition, a government must get its legislative agenda in front of the House. It must pass its economic policies. Discipline and the use of whips are therefore most important to the government. Opposition parties may be hampered by internal dissension, but they do not rise and fall based on how they vote in the chamber. If party discipline allows governments to bypass the scrutiny function it is problematic. But most often, the failure to engage in successful scrutiny is due less to party discipline and more to a lack of resources for opposition and backbench members.

Party discipline in Canada is too strong, and it is problematic. Canadians too often believe that their local members lack power and are little more than trained seals. The characterization of former prime minister Chrétien as a "friendly dictator" did little to enhance the image of the House of Commons as a responsive body (Simpson 2001). This Audit recommends a relaxing of confidence that would allow members to vote more freely on many items. Yet the link between party discipline and responsiveness is not altogether clear. Relaxing discipline will not, by itself, make members better representatives of their constituents.

Members of Parliament often find it difficult to act in a manner that pleases most of their constituents. In a strong three- or four-party system such as Canada's, often more citizens vote against a winning candidate than vote for that individual. Members of Parliament are therefore left in the unenviable position of representing a political party *plus* a riding where more than half of voters would have preferred another representative. Knowing the views of constituents is a difficult, if not impossible, task. Riding-level polling data on all important issues of the day simply do not exist in Canada, nor do members have the resources to gather such information. In the absence of quantitative information on their constituents' desires, members must rely on phone calls, letters, and visits to the constituency office, letters to the editors of local papers, mail-back portions of riding newsletters, and other sources that tend to exaggerate extreme views. Finally, MPs are often privy to information that voters do not have. Issues that may seem black and white to the electorate are often seen in various shades of grey by lawmakers. Sometimes the national interest must prevail over local concerns, despite what riding residents believe.

So how do members know if they are voting with the wishes of the majority of their constituents or simply the most vocal of them? In most cases, it is unclear. And in that majority of unclear cases, members of Parliament have the benefit of long caucus discussions to help solidify opinion within the party. On a contentious issue, party discipline becomes even more important. Members can use party discipline as a shield to fend off attacks from constituents who complain that they are not being represented in the legislature. In doing so, they protect themselves and their colleagues, thereby reinforcing party solidarity.

Unfettered free votes are not the solution to the problem of party discipline. This Audit recommends that a variation of the British three-line whip be adopted. All matters presented in a party's election platform or included in the budget should be considered matters of confidence and have a three-line whip. Any defeat on these issues would be seen as nonconfidence in the government, and an election would necessarily follow. All government members would be expected to support the party leadership on these matters.

On issues important to the government but not necessitating an election, a two-line whip would be drawn. If members could demonstrate important local considerations or matters of individual conscience, they could vote against their party without fear of recrimination. If the government were to lose the vote it would immediately be followed by a vote of confidence, on which all government members would be expected to vote with the government (the confidence vote would be a three-line whip). One-line whips would be held on matters that the government did not see as crucial to its success. Members would be encouraged to vote with the government, but again local considerations and personal convictions could trump party cohesion. Defeat on the bill would not trigger a vote of confidence or an election. The matter alone would be defeated.

In order to be successful, governments would have to announce the status of legislation early in the process, either before or upon its introduction. Just as importantly, the opposition parties would have to respect the outcome. This study found that most members in opposition do not think governments would be perceived as weak if they lost on bills that were not matters of confidence. They must stick to that conviction or risk losing the benefit of free votes. When faced with an opposition wishing to exploit perceived weaknesses, a government will quickly unite. All members must take responsibility if Canadian legislatures wish to change our understanding of confidence. Such a change must be initiated by the government (and probably at the pushing of government private members) but it must be respected by opposition MPs.

Canadian jurisdictions vary widely in the treatment of private members' public bills. Private members' business should be immune from strong party discipline; governments cannot fall on legislation that is not their own. And there is generally far less use of whips on private members' business. The problem with such bills is therefore not party discipline but rather the poor record of moving them from introduction to final passage. Some jurisdictions deal with them more than others, but no jurisdiction does so extensively or successfully. Members do not have enough opportunity to participate in legislation. This is not simply the result of a full legislative calendar, although more time could be spent on the business of private members. It would not be an insurmountable obstacle for legislatures to sit slightly longer.

More private members' business should be encouraged. This would include more votes on private members' business. Legislatures should ensure that when a private member's bill receives a second reading, it must be brought to a vote for third reading. In some Canadian legislatures, for example, a private member's bill that makes it to second reading cannot "die" on the order paper if the assembly prorogues. Other legislatures should follow this lead.

But encouraging more private members' legislation does not mean broadening its scope beyond the present restrictions. If members are to have greater flexibility to vote as they wish, and if more private members' public bills are being dealt with, then they cannot realistically expect to increase public expenditures or otherwise disrupt the economic policies of the government. The government must still be able to determine its own fiscal agenda.

Committees

Chapter 7 concluded by arguing that much of the hope for legislatures lies in committees, where representation and responsiveness are played out. Members have the greatest capacity to participate in the committee system, but often either their agenda is dictated to them or their recommendations are too easily ignored by cabinet. This leads to frustration. Committees perform valuable legislative services. If used properly committees can help to build cross-party support for public policies. This Audit has several recommendations for their use.

Legislatures should make more use of legislative or standing committees to hear from witnesses or examine proposed legislation. Committees should be encouraged to hear from witnesses on legislation, which permits healthy participation in the legislative process by the public. Although committees cannot possibly be expected to hear from every group that wishes to appear in front of them, they must open up the legislative process to the public by holding hearings. For the same reason, committees must be encouraged to travel, as many already do. The ability for interested citizens to appear before a committee is compromised when the committee does not get out of the assembly. If committees are to encourage broader public consultation and participation, travelling to communities is an effective way of reaching out.

Government-only committees should be used less. The increasing reliance on these committees both federally and provincially is a signal that governments do not value institutional opposition and accountability. Committees that do not include opposition members are exercises in evading the legislature. It is impossible to stop their use, but it should be actively discouraged.

Officers and agents who answer to legislatures should be required to make annual reports to parliamentary committees. At present this practice is not uniform. Auditors general (both federally and provincially) make annual reports and appear before committees, but they are the exception in some jurisdictions. Further, with consensus of at least a majority of members and parties, committees should be empowered to direct agents of Parliament to investigate particular policies or departments. The inability of the Public Accounts Committee, for example, to ask the auditor general to investigate a department or program neutralizes much of its authority. Requiring a double majority would help prevent this power from being abused.

Committees should be used more often at the prelegislative scrutiny stage. Bills should be sent to committees after first reading. This would allow a more open discussion and debate before parties stake out their positions on the principles of a piece of legislation at second reading. Such scrutiny has been used effectively in Canada in the past (particularly in the Senate) and more recently in Great Britain.

Often legislation is passed that allows cabinet to establish regulations. Ideally, regulations should indicate how the legislation is to be implemented and administered. In practice they can often have far greater impact on the scope and direction of legislation, and these should be reviewed by committees regularly. In 2003 the federal Standing Joint Committee for Scrutiny of Regulations was given power to "disallow" regulations that fell outside the scope of the legislation. This should serve as a model for other jurisdictions. Again a double majority would limit the abuse of such power.

Legislatures should explore the possibility that all reports on matters they investigate that represent party consensus take the form of draft government legislation. This would include matters committees choose to look at on their own and those they are asked to investigate by the government. For example, when a special committee is asked to look at an issue, its report could be first reading legislation that would become part of the government's agenda. Again, all parties or a majority of parties would have to concur with the report. Such a report and accompanying draft legislation would have no more priority than other government legislation and would involve only a one-line whip. But the implementation of committee reports would provide committees the power to engage in the initial stages of policy formation.

Finally, when committees report to the legislature, standing orders should require detailed responses from ministers. The greatest frustration faced by private members is hard work on a committee report that is quickly shelved. Detailed explanations of why a government chooses not to follow through on committee recommendations should be routine. Anything less suggests that the work of the committee is not valued. Like all other aspects of legislative life, committees can be as relevant as governments allow them to be. They are one of the most valuable assets of a legislature and should be treated as such.

Conclusion

This Audit has not been exhaustive. We have identified the three most important functions of modern legislatures: representation, scrutiny, and legislation. Like the other volumes in this series, this Audit has examined these legislative functions in terms of the three benchmarks of inclusiveness, participation, and responsiveness.

The recommendations of this Audit are not radical. Wholesale changes to our representational system are unlikely to occur in any case, especially not constitutional changes. No sane government would open up the constitutional can of worms that is Senate reform, for example. Similarly, though legislatures elected under a proportional representation system may well be more inclusive, electoral change is not likely at the federal level. Moreover, some large reforms might result in unforeseen changes. For example, relaxing party discipline too much might open the door to a mixed congressional-parliamentary system, where an executive sits in the legislature but is constantly negotiating with its own party members for support. This might lead to legislative gridlock, or even worse, the type of horse-trading and log-rolling that typifies the US Congress.

The recommendations here must therefore be realistic. The call for larger legislatures may appear radical, but it does not change the fundamental shape of our assemblies or the role of members. The move to a three-line whip would be a departure for Canadian assemblies, but it has a home in the mother of all parliaments, Westminster.

If there is a theme to this study, and to the recommendations in this chapter, it is appreciation for the men and women who serve in legislatures. In terms of constituency service, Canadians are well represented. Members are responsive to the needs of their voters. The problem with legislators in Canada is that the present structure of rules and institutions does not allow them to fully participate in many of the functions they were elected to perform. Governments that try to avoid meeting the legislature or to make it smaller only exacerbate this problem.

The best thing we can do to improve the role and status of legislatures in Canada is to let members do their job: enable legislators to legislate. Make sure we have enough of them, and allow them to study legislation, meet citizens, and closely question the executive. Any changes that facilitate these activities will only enhance the ability of elected officials to represent Canadians.

CHAPTER 8

Important reforms and ideas that legislatures in Canada should seriously consider including the following:

- All legislatures should examine the benefits of having more elected officials. In the provinces and territories larger assemblies will help in the scrutiny function. In Ottawa a larger House will encourage members to develop a parliamentary career.

- Both in the riding and in the capital, members require proper resources to provide effective representation.

- Members, and assemblies, should be more open to making better use of websites and e-mail. Members' websites should be directly accessible from the legislative website and provide nonpartisan assistance to constituents and interested voters and advocacy groups.

- Governments should relax party discipline. The British three-line whip system should be adopted and used uniformly in the House of Commons and provincial and territorial legislatures. At the same time, opposition members cannot use defeat on one- or two-line whip votes as evidence that a government is weak.

- Legislatures should make much better use of committees, including sending more bills to committee after first, not second, reading.

- Committees should be encouraged to travel more and hear from more (and more varied) Canadians.

- Officers and agents who report to Parliament should be required to make annual reports to parliamentary committees.

Discussion Questions

Chapter 1: A Democratic Audit of Canadian Legislatures

1 What are the present functions of parliamentary legislatures? What other functions should be added to these?

2 Are Parliaments losing their relevance in a modern society? If so, what are the causes?

3 If Parliaments are losing their relevance, can they be reformed or should they be replaced? If the latter, what should replace them?

4 In what way can legislatures be responsive to the public? What obstacles exist to responsiveness?

5 What are the potential drawbacks to the delegate style of representation? What about trustees?

Chapter 2: Who Represents Canadians?

1 What is mirror representation, and is it desirable?

2 Can a legislature that is not fully reflective of society properly represent the needs of a culturally diverse population?

3 What does the fact that the Senate is more representative of women and Aboriginal people than the Commons say about the electoral process in Canada? Should it make us rethink calls for an elected Senate?

4 Are lawyers best suited to passing and defeating laws? Why?

5 List the demographic, linguistic, and cultural interests that should be represented in your provincial legislature. If this assembly holds 100 seats, is it possible to achieve this goal?

Chapter 3: Roles in the Assembly

1 What are the pros and cons of electing the speaker by secret ballot? Does this provide a speaker with independence or simply raise unrealistic expectations for members of Parliament?

2 Should a speaker be allowed to run for re-election on a party ticket, or should he or she seek the support of constituents as an independent or as speaker? What are the potential consequences?

3 What are the pros and cons of prime ministers (and premiers) recruiting cabinet ministers from outside of their caucus? Does this help with the representation problems identified in Chapter 2 or simply deflate the ambitions of long-serving members?

4 How important is it for the federal cabinet to have representation from every province? Can this come at the cost of talent? If so, what can be done to offset this problem?

5 Why is the role of parliamentary secretary so frustrating for many members of Parliament? Should these individuals simply be made "junior cabinet ministers"? What might be the fallout of such a move?

Chapter 4: Constituency Work

1 Do the resources provided for constituency work constitute an unfair advantage for incumbents seeking re-election?

2 Many federal members of Parliament spend a great deal of time travelling back and forth from the capital to their home. What other professions demand this type of time and travel? Are the rewards for being a member comparable to these occupations?

3 What types of services could MPs provide citizens on a Commons-supported, nonpartisan website?

4 Think about the different policy fields covered by provincial governments versus the federal government. How do these policy areas translate into constituency work for elected officials? Which member deals with policy that more directly affects people's lives, the MLA or the MP? Do the resources provided provincial legislators match the demands of their constituency jobs?

5 Now think only of MPs, but compare the types of constituency problems dealt with by urban members to those faced by representatives of rural and northern ridings. Should members for rural ridings be provided with more resources than urban members, or less?

Chapter 5: Opportunities in the Assembly

1 What purpose was question period meant to serve? What purpose does it serve?

2 In what ways could question period be changed to make it more effective?

3 Should government backbenchers be allowed to ask questions of cabinet ministers in question period?

4 Do members' statements and other opportunities for participation help ameliorate the underrepresentation of some groups of Canadians in the Commons?

5 Can the scope of private members' bills be expanded to include legislation termed "money bills"? What would be the implications of such a move?

Chapter 6: Scrutiny and the Size of Legislatures

1 How much bigger should the House of Commons be?

2 Is the problem of size greater at the provincial/territorial level or at the federal level? Why?

3 How does the growth of new political parties exacerbate the problem of size in assemblies?

4 Could it be argued that the problem of size was not an issue as long as we had trust in our elected officials? If our leaders were held in higher regard would the problem of size disappear?

5 Do officers of Parliament assist legislators in their accountability function or do they simply obscure the lines of responsibility between cabinet ministers and legislators?

6 What criteria should exist for the creation of new officers of Parliament? Should there be a uniform reporting structure for these officers? What should their relationship be with Parliament and legislative committees?

Chapter 7: The Legislative Process

1 Is the speech from the throne a relic of bygone days that should be scrapped? What functions does the speech from the throne fulfill and how could these functions be maintained without this ritual?

2 What are the benefits of prebudgetary hearings by committees? What are the potential drawbacks of such hearings?

3 Can we distinguish between right and wrong occasions for invoking closure or time allocation? Under what conditions should governments be permitted to use either legislative tool?

4 When is party discipline desirable for members? Why are social or moral issues, such as same-sex marriages, decriminalization of marijuana, and capital punishment, more likely to be considered free votes while economic questions are more likely to be considered matters of confidence?

5 How can committees be made more effective? Should committees be able to investigate any government department within their policy area? What are the benefits and drawbacks of such a move?

Chapter 8: What Legislatures Should (and Should Not) Do

1   Is the problem of the relevancy of legislatures one of public education, or is it the fault of our legislatures and governments? Think of three changes that might make legislatures more relevant.

2   Write to your own member of Parliament to ask what he or she thinks the three most constructive reforms to the Commons would be. Now write to a member who represents a different party in a different part of the country and a different type of riding. Compare the answers. If the answers are similar, what does this say about the inability of legislatures to solve their own problems? Why can't members of Parliament simply run their own legislature?

3   Compare the problem of gridlock in the United States House of Representatives with the problem of party discipline in the Canadian House of Commons. Which one presents greater barriers to participation and responsiveness?

4   What reforms might encourage members of legislatures to pursue parliamentary, as opposed to cabinet, careers?

5   Can you add to the list of proposed reforms in this chapter?

Additional Reading

Despite the importance of legislatures as democratic bodies, there is perhaps less written on Canadian assemblies than on most other Canadian political institutions. The post-1982 era spawned an interest in the Charter and courts in the 1980s, and the wild electoral victories of 1984 and 1993 and the changes to our party system in the 1990s and early 2000s gave rise to increased interest in parties. As a result, legislatures have been less studied by academics, but not ignored. The following admittedly brief list of further readings is broadly outlined along the themes of each chapter.

The best text on Canada's Parliament remains the 1987 book by Charles Edward Selwyn Franks, *The Parliament of Canada.* While it is now somewhat dated, it provides a wonderful overview of the role and functions of both the House of Commons and the Senate. Philip Norton's book *The Commons in perspective* (1981) provides a similar treatment of the lower house at Westminster. For an excellent article on the state of the Canadian House of Commons, be sure to check out Jennifer Smith's "Democracy and the Canadian House of Commons at the millennium," published in *Canadian Public Administration* in 1999. Many good articles and books have been written on the problems facing legislatures. Donald Savoie's 1999 book, *Governing from the centre,* paints a rather unfriendly portrait of the concentration of power under Jean Chrétien, as does Jeffrey Simpson's 2001 book, *The friendly dictatorship.*

There are a number of excellent studies on representation and assemblies in Canada. The work of Jerome Black in the *Canadian Parliamentary Review* on "Ethnoracial minorities in the House of Commons" (2002a) is the most up-to-date examination of minority group representation in federal house. His chapter in Everitt and O'Neill's *Citizen politics* (2002b) makes a coherent argument that more ethnic diversity in the Commons would increase the level of substantive representation in the chamber. In 2003 Manon Tremblay and Linda Trimble published an edited volume titled *Women and electoral politics in Canada,* which contains a number of excellent chapters on gender and representation. Their own chapter in the book provides a concise sociodemographic profile of female politicians in Canada. Jerome Black has a nice chapter in this book as well, looking specifically at minority women MPs during much of the Chrétien era.

Without doubt the best book on cabinet ministers is the Graham White (2005) volume in this Democratic Audit series. Gary Levy has written several good articles on the role of the speaker. His "A night to remember: The first election of a speaker by secret ballot" in the winter 1986 *Canadian Parliamentary Review* is a wonderfully written account of John Fraser's historic election. In the spring 1998 edition of the same journal, Levy details how the speakership has developed both provincially and federally, in "The evolving speakership." Peter Dobell is correctly regarded as an expert on the role of members of Parliament. Anyone interested in the problems facing parliamentary secretaries should take a careful look at his 2001 study for the Institute for Research on Public Policy titled *Parliamentary secretaries: The consequences of constant rotation*. David Hutchison has a nice article that examines "Parliamentary secretaries in the 36th Parliament" in the spring 2000 issue of *Canadian Parliamentary Review*.

The term "home style" was coined by American political scientist Richard Fenno in a book of the same name. The book, published in 1978, remains one of the great contributions to understanding how elected officials work in their districts and the challenges they face. Another good comparative book is *Back from Westminster: British members of Parliament and their constituencies* (1993), in which Philip Norton and David Wood discuss the increasing importance of constituency work to British MPs. My own 1997 book, *Mr. Smith goes to Ottawa: Life in the House of Commons,* concentrates on the legislative life of members, but does devote considerable space to understanding how they approach local service and their enjoyment of this work. There has naturally been less work done on members and new technology, but two studies in particular focus on Canadian federal legislators and the web. Jonathan Malloy's *To better serve Canadians: How technology is changing the relationship between members of Parliament and public servants* was published by the Institute of Public Administration of Canada in December 2003. Harold Jansen and Melanee Thomas presented a wonderful paper at the 2003 annual meeting of the Canadian Political Science Association called "www.mp.ca: Members of Parliament and constituency communication using the World Wide Web." Both are worth a close look.

In 2000 Robert Marleau and Camille Montpetit published a lengthy book titled *House of Commons procedure and practice.* Do not let the title throw you off. This book is well written and full of insights into the workings of the House and interesting stories about speaker's rulings and the antics of members. If it had been called *Everything you wanted to know about the House of Commons but were afraid to ask,* more undergraduates would read it on Saturday nights. For those interested in how the present parliamentary calendar and workday developed, this book is fabulous.

During the period 1974-93 Canada had a three-party political system. That was shattered in 1993, and by 1997 there were five recognized parties in the Canadian House of Commons. A Parliamentary Perspectives paper I wrote in 1998 titled *It's awfully crowded here: Adjusting to the five party House of Commons* outlines some of the challenges faced by the so-called pizza parliament.

For more information on private members' business, the reflections of Clifford Lincoln and other members on parliamentary reform, aptly titled "Members look at parliamentary reform" (2001), makes good reading. Suhas Deshpande's article "Removing barriers to private members' business" in the spring 1995 volume of *Canadian Parliamentary Review* is also quite good.

Very little has been written on the question of the size of Canadian legislatures. John Courtney's work for the Macdonald Commission, "The size of Canada's Parliament: An assessment of the implications of a larger House of Commons" (1985), remains the best work in this area. There has been even less done on the question of officers of Parliament, though work on individual offices is more easily found (for example, see Sharon Sutherland's 1986 article, "The politics of audit: The federal office of the auditor-general in comparative perspective"). Officers of Parliament have become an area of increasing interest, particularly with the recent growth of these offices at the provincial level. Peter Dobell produced a paper for the Parliamentary Centre's Occasional Papers on Parliamentary Government in September 2002 called *Agencies that report to Parliament*. In this work, four officers of Parliament discuss such matters as how they interact with Parliament and their independence from the government. The best comparative work in this area was produced by Oonagh Gay for the British House of Commons Library. The report, *Officers of Parliament: A comparative perspective*, was published in October 2003.

The Parliament of Canada website (www.parl.gc.ca) is a wonderful resource for students. The site provides links to papers written for the Parliamentary Library, information on the Commons calendar, and basic information on how Parliament functions.

Most standard Canadian government texts provide a good overview of the legislative process. A good two-page guide to how a bill becomes law can be found in Keith Archer et al., *Parameters of power: Canada's political institutions* (2002). While far more simple than the American process, there is more to passing a bill than meets the eye.

Jonathan Malloy has a very good article that touches on party discipline and reform during the Chrétien years, aptly called "The House of Commons under the Chrétien government" (2003). For a discussion of Chrétien's so-called lame duck period during his last year in office and how some backbencher Liberals finally rebelled see my "The rebels find a cause: House of Commons reform in the Chrétien era" in the summer 2004 issue of *Review of Constitutional Studies*.

Works Cited

Legislative Websites

House of Assembly of Newfoundland and Labrador, www.gov.nf.ca/hoa
Legislative Assembly of Alberta, www.assembly.ab.ca
Legislative Assembly of British Columbia, www.legis.gov.bc.ca
Legislative Assembly of Manitoba, www.gov.mb.ca/leg-asmb/index.html
Legislative Assembly of New Brunswick, www.gnb.ca/legis
Legislative Assembly of the Northwest Territories, www.assembly.gov.nt.ca
Legislative Assembly of Nova Scotia, www.gov.ns.ca/legislature
Legislative Assembly of Nunavut, www.assembly.nu.ca
Legislative Assembly of Ontario, www.ontla.on.ca
Legislative Assembly of Prince Edward Island, www.assembly.pe.ca
Legislative Assembly of Saskatchewan, www.legassembly.sk.ca
Legislative Assembly of the Yukon Territory, www.gov.yk.ca/leg-assembly
National Assembly of Quebec, www.assnat.qc.ca
Parliament of Canada, www.parl.gc.ca

Books and Articles

Archer, Keith, Roger Gibbins, Rainer Knopff, Heather MacIvor, and Leslie Pal. 2002. *Parameters of power: Canada's political institutions.* Scarborough, ON: Thomson Nelson.

Atkinson, Michael M. 1994. What kind of democracy do Canadians want? *Canadian Journal of Political Science* 27(4): 717-46.

Atkinson, Michael, and David Docherty. 2004. Parliament and political success in Canada. In *Canadian politics in the 21st century,* 6th ed., ed. Michael Whittington and Glen Williams, 5-30. Scarborough, ON: Thomson Nelson.

Australia. House of Representatives. 2002. Opportunities for private members. House of Representatives Info Sheet no. 6. April.

Bagehot, Walter. [1867] 1961. *The English constitution.* London: Oxford University Press.

Bashevkin, Sylvia. 1985. *Toeing the lines: Women and party politics in English Canada.* Toronto: University of Toronto Press.

Bennett, Carolyn. 2002. 16 January. Cabinet shuffle: Thrilled about Bill Graham, disappointed by dropping percentage of women in cabinet. <www.carolynbennett.ca>. (1 September 2002).

Birch, Anthony. 1964. *Representative and responsible government.* Toronto: University of Toronto Press.

Black, Jerome. 2002a. Ethnoracial minorities in the House of Commons. *Canadian Parliamentary Review* 25(1).

—. 2002b. Representation in the Parliament of Canada: The case of ethnoracial minorities. In *Citizen politics: Research and theory in Canadian political behaviour,* ed. Joanna Everitt and Brenda O'Neill, 355-72. Toronto: Oxford University Press.

Blaikie, Bill. 1994. The status of small parties in the Canadian House of Commons. *Canadian Parliamentary Review* 17(3): 29-32.

Boyle, Theresa. 2001. "I have to name names," Guzzo insists. *Toronto Star,* 29 May, A7.

Burke, Edmund. 1834. Speech on arrival at Bristol. 3 November 1774. *The works of Edmund Burke.* Vol. 1, 176-80. London: Holdesworth and Ball.

Cain, Brian, John Ferejohn, and Morris Fiorina. 1987. The personal vote: Constituency service and electoral independence. Cambridge, MA: Harvard University Press.

Cairns, Alan C. 1992. *Charter versus federalism: The dilemmas of constitutional reform.* Montreal: McGill-Queen's University Press.

Cameron, David. 1995. Shifting the burden: Liberal policy for post-secondary education. In *How Ottawa spends 1995-96: Mid-life crisis,* ed. Susan D. Philips, 159-84. Ottawa: Carleton University Press.

Campbell, Robert M., and Leslie A. Pal. 1991. *The real worlds of Canadian politics: Cases in process and policy.* 2nd ed. Peterborough, ON: Broadview Press.

Canadian Election Study. 2000. <www.fas.umontreal.ca/pol/ces-eec/index.html>. (21 April 2004).

Canadian Parliamentary Guides. 1941, 1971, 1990-2004. Ottawa.

Carty, R. Kenneth, William Cross, and Lisa Young. 2000. *Rebuilding Canadian party politics.* Vancouver: UBC Press.

Clarke, Harold, Jane Jenson, Larry LeDuc, and Jon Pammett. 1996. *Absent mandate: Electoral politics in an era of restructuring.* 3rd ed. Scarborough, ON: Gage Publishing.

Congressional Research Service. 1999. Salaries and allowance: The Congress. Report for the Congress. <www.house.gov/rules>. (30 August 2004).

Courtney, John. 1974. On the passing of politicians' occupations. *Dalhousie Law Review* 54 (Spring): 81-93.

—. 1985. The size of Canada's Parliament: An assessment of the implications of a larger House of Commons. In *Institutional reforms for representative government,* ed. Peter Aucoin, 1-39. Royal Commission on the Economic Union and Development Prospects for Canada, research vol. 38. Toronto: University of Toronto Press.

—. 1995. *Do conventions matter? Choosing national party leaders in Canada.* Montreal: McGill-Queen's University Press.

—. 2004. *Elections*. Vancouver: UBC Press.

Cross, William. 2004. *Political parties*. Vancouver: UBC Press.

Crossing Boundaries National Council. 2002. MP website study results. <www.crossingboundaries.ca/index>. (30 August 2004).

Davidson, Dianne. 1995. The powers of parliamentary committees. *Canadian Parliamentary Review* 18(1): 12-15.

Delacourt, Susan. 1997. How an anonymous telephone call led to crisis on Parliament Hill. *Globe and Mail*, 28 April, A15.

Deshpande, Suhas. 1995. Removing barriers to private members' business. *Canadian Parliamentary Review* 18(1): 23-5.

Dobell, Peter C. 2001. *Parliamentary secretaries: The consequences of constant rotation*. Policy Matters series vol. 2, no. 4. Ottawa: Institute for Research on Public Policy. <www.irpp.org>.

—. 2002. *Agencies that report to Parliament*. Occasional Papers on Parliamentary Government, no. 14-15 (September). Ottawa: Parliamentary Centre. <www.parlcent.ca>. (1 October 2002).

Docherty, David C. 1997. *Mr. Smith goes to Ottawa: Life in the House of Commons*. Vancouver: UBC Press.

—. 1998. *It's awfully crowded here: Adjusting to the five party House of Commons*. Parliamentary Perspectives series, vol. 2. Ottawa: Canadian Study of Parliament Group. <www.studyparliament.ca>.

—. 1999. Parliamentarians and government accountability. In *Public administration and policy: governing in challenging times,* ed. Martin Westmacott and Hugh Mellon, 38-52. Scarborough, ON: Prentice-Hall.

—. 2002a. The Canadian Senate: Chamber of sober reflection or loony cousin best not talked about. *Journal of Legislative Studies* 8 (3): 27-48.

—. 2002b. Citizens and legislators: Different views on representation. In *Value change and governance in Canada,* ed. Neil Nevitte, 165-206. Toronto: University of Toronto Press.

—. 2002c. Political careers in Canada. In *Citizen politics: Research and theory in Canadian political behaviour,* ed. Joanna Everitt and Brenda O'Neill, 338-54. Toronto: Oxford University Press.

—. 2004. The rebels find a cause: House of Commons reform in the Chrétien era. *Review of Constitutional Studies* 9, 1-2 (Summer): 283-302.

Docherty, David, and Graham White. 1999. *Throwing the rascals out: Defeat and re-election in the Canadian provinces*. Paper delivered at the annual meeting of the Midwest Political Science Association, Chicago, April.

Dominion Bureau of Statistics. 1946. Gainfully occupied, 14 years of age and over by industry, selected occupations, and sex, for Canada and the provinces, 1941. *Eighth census of Canada, 1941*. Vol. 7. Ottawa: Ministry of Trade and Commerce.

Dyck, Rand. 1996. *Provincial politics in Canada*. 2nd ed. Scarborough, ON: Prentice-Hall.

Elections Canada. 2002. Representation in the House of Commons of Canada. <www.elections.ca.>. (26 January 2004).

Eulau, Heinz. 1978. Changing views of representation. In *The politics of representation: Continuities in theory and research,* ed. J. Wahlke and A. Abramowitz, 31-53. Beverly Hills, CA: Sage Publications.

Everitt, Joanna. 2002. Gender gaps on social welfare issues: Why do women care? In *Citizen politics: Research and theory in Canadian political behaviour,* ed. Joanna Everitt and Brenda O'Neill, 110-25. Toronto: Oxford University Press.

Fenno, Richard. 1978. *Home style: House members in their districts*. Boston: Little, Brown.

Francoli, Paco, and Mike Scandiffio. 2002. Scrambling' Grits working on Commons reform package. *Hill Times,* 11 November, 1.

Franks, Charles Edward Selwyn. 1987. *The Parliament of Canada*. Toronto: University of Toronto Press.

Gauthier, Jean-Robert. 1993. Accountability, committees and Parliament. *Canadian Parliamentary Review* 16(2): 7-9.

Gay, Oonagh. 2003. *Officers of Parliament: A comparative perspective*. Research paper 03/77, October. Westminster, UK: House of Commons Library. <www.parliament.uk/commons/lib/research/rp2003/rp03-077.pdf>. (17 May 2004).

Glenn, John E. 1997. Parliamentary assistant? Patronage or apprenticeship. In *Fleming's Canadian legislatures,* ed. Robert Fleming and John E. Glenn, 48-59. Toronto: University of Toronto Press.

Hibbing, John. 1991. *Congressional careers: contours of life in the US House of Representatives*. Chapel Hill: University of North Carolina Press.

House of Commons. 1982. Third report of the Special Committee on Standing Orders and Procedure. *Minutes of Proceedings and Evidence,* 4 November, no. 7.

—. 1994. *Debates*. 1st session, 35th Parliament. Vols. 9 and 10.

—. 1998. *Debates*. 1st session, 36th Parliament. Nos. 149-62.

—. 2001. *Committees: A practical guide*. 6th ed. Ottawa. <www.parl.gc.ca/InfoCom/documents/GuidePratique/TitlePage-e.html>. (26 May 2004).

—. 2002a. *Debates*. 30 September 2002.

—. 2002b. *Performance report 2001-2002: House of Commons administration*. Ottawa. <www.parl.gc.ca/information/about/process>. (26 May 2004).

Howard, Ross. 1989. Wilson must resign, opposition insists. *Globe and Mail,* 27 April, A1.

Howe, Paul, and David Northrup. 2000. *Strengthening Canadian democracy: The views of Canadians*. Policy Matters series vol. 1, no. 5. Ottawa: Institute for Research on Public Policy.

Hutchison, David Gamache. 2000. Parliamentary secretaries in the 36th Parliament. *Canadian Parliamentary Review* 23(1): 20-8.

Irvine, William. 1982. Does the candidate make a difference? The macro-politics and micro-politics of getting elected in Canada. *Canadian Journal of Political Science* 15(4): 755-85.

Jacobson, Gary, and Samuel Kernell. 1983. *Strategy and choice in congressional elections.* New Haven, CT: Yale University Press.

Jansen, Harold, and Melanee Thomas. 2003. www.mp.ca: Members of Parliament and constituency communication using the World Wide Web. Paper presented at the annual meeting of the Canadian Political Science Association, Halifax, 1 June.

Joyal, Serge. 2000. The Senate you thought you knew. Paper presented at the annual meeting of the Canadian Political Science Association, Quebec City, July.

King, Anthony. 1981. The rise of the career politician in Great Britain — and its consequences. *British Journal of Political Science* 11: 249-85.

Laghi, Brian. 2002a. Rivals accuse Day of threatening caucus. *Globe and Mail,* 1 March, A8.

—. 2002b. The sudden fall of two heavyweights: Contract awarded to former girlfriend was only one of many errors but it created opportunity for dismissal. *Globe and Mail,* 27 May, A7.

Leblanc, Daniel. 2002. The sudden fall of two heavyweights: Minister's integrity standards were set high when in opposition and now he's paying the price, Tory says. *Globe and Mail,* 27 May, A7.

Levy, Gary. 1986. A night to remember: The first election of a speaker by secret ballot. *Canadian Parliamentary Review* 9(4): 10-14.

—. 1998. The evolving speakership. *Canadian Parliamentary Review* 21(2): 7-11.

Liberal Party of Canada. 1993. *Creating opportunity: The Liberal plan for Canada.* Ottawa: Liberal Party.

Lincoln, Clifford, Rob Merrifield, Stéphane Bergeron, Lorne Nystrom, and Bill Casey. 2001. Members look at parliamentary reform. *Canadian Parliamentary Review* 24(2): 11-17.

Lindquist, Evert A. 1985. *Consultation and budget secrecy: Reforming the process of creating budgets in the federal government.* Ottawa: Conference Board of Canada.

Loewenberg, Gerhard, and Samuel Patterson. 1979. *Comparing legislatures.* Lanham, MD: University Press of America.

Loomis, Burdett. 1988. *The new American politician: Ambition, entrepreneurship and the changing face of political life.* New York: Basic Books.

McCarthy, Shawn. 2002a. MacAulay resigns but admits no fault. *Globe and Mail,* 23 October, A1 and A4.

—. 2002b. PM plans old-time activism. *Globe and Mail,* 1 October, A1 and A5.

—. 2002c. Key vote fractures Liberals. *Globe and Mail,* 6 November, A1.

McInnes, David. 1999. *Taking it to the hill.* Ottawa: University of Ottawa Press.

MacKay, Robert A. 1963. *The unreformed Senate of Canada,* revised and reprinted. Toronto: McClelland and Stewart.

Mackie, Richard. 2001. MPP defends plan to name names. *Globe and Mail,* 30 May, A6.

—. 2003a. Eves to shun legislature in TV budget. *Globe and Mail,* 13 March, A1 and A7.

—. 2003b. Made-for-TV budget draws more fire. *Globe and Mail,* 18 March, A12.

Malloy, Jonathan. 1996. Reconciling expectations and reality in the House of Commons committees: The case of the 1989 GST inquiry. *Canadian Public Administration* 39(3): 314-35.

—. 2003a. The House of Commons under the Chrétien government. In *How Ottawa Spends,* ed. Bruce Doern, 59-71. Toronto: Oxford University Press.

—. 2003b. *To better serve Canadians: How technology is changing the relationship between members of Parliament and public servants.* New Directions series no. 9. Toronto: Institute of Public Administration of Canada.

Marleau, Robert. 2000. Some thoughts on the future of parliamentary committees. *Canadian Parliamentary Review* 23(2): 24-6.

Marleau, Robert, and Camille Montpetit. 2000. *House of Commons procedure and practice.* Ottawa: House of Commons and Chenelière and McGraw-Hill.

Massicotte, Louis. 1989. Quebec: The successful combination of French culture and British institutions. In *Provincial and territorial legislatures in Canada,* ed. Gary Levy and Graham White, 68-89. Toronto: University of Toronto Press.

Mayhew, David R. 1974. *Congress: The electoral connection.* New Haven, CT: Yale University Press.

Mellon, Hugh. 1993. *Duelling budgetary beliefs — Langdon versus Rae: Party discipline in the NDP.* Paper delivered at the annual meeting of the Canadian Political Science Association, Ottawa.

Moncrief, Gary. 1994. Professionalization and careerism in Canadian provincial assemblies: Comparison to U.S. state legislatures. *Legislative Studies Quarterly* 9(1): 33-48.

Morton, William Lewis. 1967. *The Progressive Party in Canada.* Toronto: University of Toronto Press.

Murray, Lowell. 2000. MPs, political parties, and parliamentary democracies. *Isuma* 1(2): 103-6.

Norton, Philip. 1981. *The Commons in perspective.* Oxford: Martin Robinson Press.

—. 2000. Parliament in transition. In *United Kingdom governance,* ed. Robert Pyper and Lynton Robins, 82-106. London: Macmillan.

Norton, Phillip, and David Wood. 1993. *Back from Westminster: British members of Parliament and their constituencies.* Lexington: University of Kentucky Press.

Ontario. Legislative Assembly. 1997. *Hansard.* 22 June and 18 November.

—. 1999. *Standing orders.* November.

Ontario. Legislative Assembly. Standing Committee on the Legislative Assembly. 2002. *Report on enhancing the role of the private member.* December.

Pelletier, Yves. 2000. *Time allocation in the House of Commons: Silencing parliamentary democracy or effective time management.* Parliamentary intern paper. Ottawa: Institute on Governance.

Persichilli, Angelo. 2002. Political parties must be "democratized," not Parliament. *Hill Times,* 11 November, 4.

Pitkin, Hanna. 1967. *The concept of representation.* London: University of California Press.

Power, Charles G. 1957. The career politician: The changing role of the MP. *Queen's Quarterly* 43(4): 478-90.

Prince Edward Island. Legislative Assembly. 1998. *Standing orders.* March.

Radwanski, Adam. 2002. Chrétien's leadership strategy gives loyalists nothing to do. *Hill Times,* 12 August, 1-3.

Rice, James. 1995. Redesigning welfare: The abandonment of a national commitment. In *How Ottawa spends 1995-96: Mid-life crisis,* ed. Susan D. Philips, 185-209. Ottawa: Carleton University Press.

Riddell, Peter. 2000. *Parliament under Blair.* London: Politico Publishing.

Robertson, James R. 1991. *The standing orders of the House of Commons: Highlights of the 1991 amendments.* Background paper 256E (May). Ottawa: Library of Parliament Research Branch.

Royal Commission on Aboriginal Peoples. 1996. *Looking forward, looking back.* Ottawa: Ministry of Supply and Services.

Royal Commission on Electoral Reform and Party Financing. 1991. *Reforming electoral democracy: Final report.* Vol. 3. Toronto: Dundurn Press.

Royal Commission on the Economic Union and Development Prospects for Canada. 1984. *Report.* Vol. 3. Ottawa: Queen's Printers.

Rush, Michael. 2001. *The role of the member of Parliament since 1868: From gentlemen to players.* Oxford: Oxford University Press.

Saskatchewan. Legislative Assembly. 2003. *Rules and Procedures of Saskatchewan Assembly.*

Sauvé v. Canada [Chief Electoral Officer]. (2002) SCC 68.

Savoie, Donald. 1999. *Governing from the centre.* Toronto: University of Toronto Press.

Scoffield, Heather. 2002. Eggleton's awful day unfolded in a hurry. *Globe and Mail,* 28 May, A1 and A4.

Searing, Donald. 1994. *Westminster's world: Understanding political roles.* Cambridge, MA: Harvard University Press.

Sgro, Judy. 2002. Canada's urban strategy: A blueprint for action. Final report of the Prime Minister's Task Force on Urban Issues. November. <www.liberal. parl.gc.ca>. (26 January 2004).

Silk, Paul, and Rhodri Walters. 1995. *How Parliament works.* London: Longman Books.

Simpson, Jeffrey. 1980. *Discipline of power: The Conservative interlude and the Liberal restoration.* Toronto: Personal Library Publishers.

—. 2002. *The friendly dictatorship.* Toronto: McClelland and Stewart.

Smith, David. 1997. The federal cabinet in Canadian politics. In *Canadian politics in the 1990s,* ed. Michael Whittington and Glen Williams, 282-301. Toronto: Nelson Canada.

Smith, Jennifer. 1998. Responsible government and democracy. In *Taking stock of 150 years of responsible democracy in Canada,* ed. Leslie Seidle and Louis Massicotte, 19-50. Ottawa: Canadian Study of Parliament Group.

—. 1999. Democracy and the Canadian House of Commons at the millennium. *Canadian Public Administration* 42(4): 398-421.

Squire, Peverill. 1988. Career opportunities and membership stability in legislatures. *Legislative Studies Quarterly* 13(1): 65-82.

Statistics Canada. 1973. Bulletin 1.2-2. Vol. 1, part 2. March.

—. 1974. Labour force, 15 years and over, by detailed occupation and sex, for Canada and provinces. *Occupations.* 1971 Census. Ottawa: Ministry of Industry, Trade, and Commerce.

—. 2002. Experienced labour force 15 years and over by occupation, sex, and province. <www.statcan.ca>. (1 June 2004).

Stewart, Ian. 1989. Prince Edward Island: A damn queer parliament. In *Provincial and territorial legislatures in Canada,* ed. Gary Levy and Graham White, 13-28. Toronto: University of Toronto Press.

Strickland, Pat. 2001. *Election of a Commons speaker.* Parliamentary research paper (March). Westminster, UK: House of Commons Library, Parliament and Constitution Centre.

Sutherland, Sharon. 1986. The politics of audit: The federal office of the auditor-general in comparative perspective. *Canadian Public Administration* 29(1): 118-48.

Taber, Jane. 2001. Deputy voted speaker after five ballots. *National Post,* 30 January, A1.

—. 2002. Fundraising bill upsets PM's caucus. *Globe and Mail,* 30 January, A4.

Thomas, Paul. 1998. *Party caucuses: Behind closed doors.* Parliamentary Perspectives series no. 1. Ottawa: Canadian Study of Parliament Group. <www. studyparliament.ca>.

—. 2003. The past, present, and future of officers of Parliament. *Canadian Public Administration* 46(3): 287-314.

Thompson, Andrea. 2001. MPP delays decision to identify pedophiles. *Toronto Star,* 31 May, A7.

Tremblay, Manon, and Linda Trimble, eds. 2003. *Women and electoral politics in Canada.* Toronto: Oxford University Press.

Walsh, R.R. 2002. By the numbers: A statistical survey of private member's bills. *Canadian Parliamentary Review* 25(1): 29-33.

Ward, Norman. 1987. *Dawson's the Government of Canada.* 6th edition. Toronto: University of Toronto Press.

White, Graham. 1989. *The Ontario legislature: A political analysis.* Toronto: University of Toronto Press.

—. 2005. *Cabinets and first ministers.* Vancouver: UBC Press.

Young, Lisa. 1991. Legislative turnover and the election of women to the Canadian House of Commons. In *Women in Canadian Politics: Toward equity in representation,* ed. Kathy Megyery, 81-100. Royal Commission on Electoral Reform and Party Financing, research vol. 6. Toronto: Dundurn Press.

—. 1997a. Gender equal legislatures: Evaluating the proposed Nunavut electoral system. *Canadian Public Policy* 23(3): 306-15.

—. 1997b. Women in the House of Commons: The mandate of difference. In *In the Presence of Women,* ed. Linda Trimble and Jane Arscott. Toronto: Harcourt Brace.

INDEX

A master index to all volumes in the Canadian Democratic Audit series can be found at www.ubcpress.ca/readingroom/audit/index.

Printed and bound in Canada by Friesens

Copy editor: Sarah Wight

Text design: Peter Ross, Counterpunch

Typesetter: Artegraphica Design Co. Ltd.

Proofreader: Gail Copeland

Indexer: Noeline Bridge